Heartfelt

A MOMENT IN TIME

JOY KIMLER

Heartfelt
Copyright © 2022 by Joy Kimler

All rights reserved. No part of this publication
may be reproduced, distributed, or transmitted
in any form or by any means, including
photocopying, recording, or other electronic
or mechanical methods, without the prior
written permission of the author, except
in the case of brief quotations embodied
in critical reviews and certain other non-
commercial uses permitted by copyright law.

Tellwell Talent
www.tellwell.ca

ISBN
978-0-2288-8046-2 (Paperback)

Table of Contents

Author's Note

In my sixty-seven years, I have been a horse enthusiast, a competitor, a trainer and a coach. It is my experience that you cannot bring horse people together without the conversation shifting to one special horse in their life that stood out amongst the rest. That is what *Heartfelt* is all about.

Heartfelt tells the stories of Canadians who rose to the top of their particular discipline in the horse world. I chose stories from different disciplines so the book would appeal to many equestrians. As for most athletes, the road to success for equestrians is not always smooth and money is often tight. Horses are not always perfect, but they have heart and the ability to learn.

Heartfelt is written for horse/animal enthusiasts of all ages. I anticipate those as young as twelve and as old as ninety-two will enjoy each story. The book is presented in a straightforward reading style designed to relay biographical information and occasionally tug on your heartstrings.

Introduction

The idea of writing *Heartfelt* came from discussions had around a campfire: a group of adults talking about their experiences with horses they had owned in their life. Most of the stories were funny, engaging and familiar, as we all identified with the situations. I wanted to start telling these stories from the perspective of individuals who had reached great heights in their particular discipline.

The contributors to this book include former Canadian Olympians, a respected cow boss, Western riders, English riders, and those trained to drive carriages around obstacles at breathtaking speeds. There is something in this book for everyone.

When you watch a polished horse person performing, you might think it looks easy to buy a horse, love it, ride it and do well in competitions. This book reveals the challenges faced on the way to that performance. The road to success is not always easy, and a great deal of training, commitment, and of course, money—lots and lots of money—is required to reach one's goal.

In this book, you will learn about various training methods, the ups and downs, the wins and losses, but there is a common thread in all the stories included here: the love for the horse. Human and horse partnerships are formed through hard work, patience and understanding. You will read stories lauding the athleticism and cooperation of a creature that can just as quickly hurt you and defy your requests.

Each story will bring you closer to what life is like when you bond with a horse. In the horse community, there are always people happy to help you on your way. A connection with a horse is a lifetime experience, one that keeps teaching you with every new horse you let into your life.

I chose the title of this book, *Heartfelt*, many years ago. It interests me that the subtitle's meaning was not revealed to me until I had completed editing most of the stories. I have met and know most, though not all, of the people showcased in this book. I met them between1970 and 1979. It was my moment in time when I awoke to the competitive horse world in Canada. The quality of horses bred and shown was rising, and athletes were being identified on the world stage. All I could say was, "WOW! How exciting."

I worked for Jim Day and Hugh Graham. This book was a great opportunity to reconnect with Hugh. I was eighteen when I met him at Sam-Son Farm. One of my Humber College Horsemanship program teachers was

Liz Ashton. I took clinics with Nick Holmes-Smith. I followed Robin Hahn's competitions; then at a later date, he coached me in Three-Day Eventing. Larry Brinker was a judge at some of my competitions. The rest of the book's contributors, like Jonathan Field, I came to appreciate with the evolving world of natural horsemanship. I had the privilege to sit with Orville and Anita Unrau, and Leslie Reid, enthralled by their stories. Miles Kingdon and Lisa Coulter graciously allowed me to tell their stories. You will find connections among this group as they helped one another grow.

Part of owning a horse often ends in selling that same horse. It may seem odd for those who love animals to have this incredible connection, then pass the animal off to someone else. Except for the wealthy, if you wish to continue riding and growing, the sale of one horse finances the purchase of another. Horses are expensive to keep. You put hard work into training an individual, and eventually, the horse reaches its physical and sometimes mental limit. If you can match that horse up with someone eager to learn, both horse and rider benefit. That horse is loved and appreciated while not being asked to do tasks outside its limits. It is tough to let go of a partner and friend, but that is how it must be if you aspire to greater heights. I have let go of many partners and cried like a baby. The solace comes when the new owner showers their new horse with love and praise while gaining some success themselves.

As a coach, I often told my students, "You will learn a little about horses and a lot about yourself." Horses are a physical window to your soul. What you feel, the horse will project. You have to change your behaviour to fit the personality of the horse you are training. You will see that scenario played out over and over again in this book.

As Nick Holmes-Smith would say, "Enough talk, let's go." In our case, "Enough talk, let's get reading."

Spot on With Spot Check
Hugh Graham and Spot Check

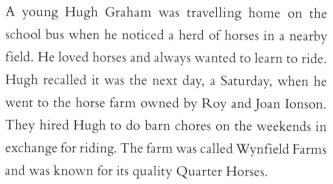

A young Hugh Graham was travelling home on the school bus when he noticed a herd of horses in a nearby field. He loved horses and always wanted to learn to ride. Hugh recalled it was the next day, a Saturday, when he went to the horse farm owned by Roy and Joan Ionson. They hired Hugh to do barn chores on the weekends in exchange for riding. The farm was called Wynfield Farms and was known for its quality Quarter Horses.

Peter Van Eerd rode and trained horses for the farm and also rode bulls at the rodeo. He was an inspiration for Hugh and taught him what he knew about steer riding. Hugh continued improving his horse skills while becoming proficient at staying on steers. At thirteen years old he was competing at the rodeos, and in 1963 at the age of fourteen, he won the Junior Steer Rider Championship for the year.

Fred Mackenzie replaced Peter Van Eerd at the Wynfield farm. Fred's specialty was calf roping. At one memorable event, Fred roped the calf's legs together in ten seconds, earning him the nickname "Ten-flat Mac." There was no better man then Fred to teach Hugh how to rope. He became passionate and practiced on everything he could find, mainly bales of hay. Before long, Hugh was calf roping at the rodeos, and in 1965 he won the Calf Roping Championship for the year. Hugh says, "I missed a lot of school but I never missed a rodeo."

Hugh's learning would continue with Milo Hetherington being hired at Wynfield Farms. Milo, in his early years, trained horses for the circus, so his horsemanship skills were excellent. Milo's position at the farm included buying, training and selling horses. He taught Hugh patience and the significance of repetition. Milo and Hugh had a great partnership where Milo would do the groundwork, and Hugh would do the riding.

Amidst all the success, in August of 1968, a horse fell on Hugh in Gerry, New York, and Hugh suffered a broken leg which sidelined his rodeo career. Instead of wasting time, Hugh decided to return to school and become a teacher. A year went by, but he was not satisfied with his career path. Hugh left his teaching position and found Milo at Style Acres, where he went back to riding horses. This is what he really wanted to do.

Milo was contacted by Jim Day at Sam-Son Farm concerning a horse that bucked everyone off. Sam-Son Farm was owned by Ernie Samuel, who earned his money running a competitive steel and aluminum distribution business. Still, his passion was horses. Ernie employed Jim Day, a show jumping Olympian. Jimmy managed the show barn and was involved with many aspects of running the farm. Sam-Son knew about Milo's reputation and sent the dangerous horse to be "fixed." Hugh Graham took over training the bucking horse until it could be ridden. Upon returning the horse to Sam-Son Farm, it immediately bucked off the first person who attempted to ride it. The horse was worthwhile but needed a competent rider. That rider would be Hugh Graham.

Hugh Graham:

I accepted the job at Sam-Son Farm in 1969. The main part of my work was to break and train young racehorses. I was reunited with "Bronc," the bucking horse, and continued with his training.

In the fall of 1969, Alan Clarkson showed up with a four-year-old, sixteen-hands-one-inch, unbacked Clydesdale/Hackney gelding named Spot Check. Jim Day put the horse on a lunge line and popped him over a jump. He raised the jump to see what this young horse could do. After three impressive jumps, to say the least, Jim asked the selling price. "Twelve hundred dollars," Alan stated. Jimmy said, "Sold," and Sam-Son Farm became the owner of another potential showjumper.

What impressed us about this young horse was his technique over the jumps. He jerked his knees together, rounded his back and kicked his butt high. All things you look for in a jumper. His temperament was more like a pet, so he was easy enough, but he was a sensitive ride, so you needed to know what you were doing.

On January 1, 1970, I was riding full-time. I rode everything—sale horses, Jimmy's jumpers, the young Thoroughbred stock—all on an English saddle. It was my job to start Spot Check. I taught him to accept the bridle, saddle, a rider, learn to turn, walk, trot and canter, which took about thirty days. The rest of that year and all of Spot Check's five-year-old year were spent training him to jump under Jim Day's supervision. I had much to learn. Jim Day was a talented rider and had a smooth way of riding; I watched Jimmy riding while paying close attention to everything he did. I asked questions and practiced what I saw.

When winter came, I started going to schooling shows on the indoor circuit. That was my first taste of jumper competition. In the spring, I travelled to the Joker's Hill Equestrian Centre schooling show and won the Jumper Stake class on Spot Check, beating Jimmy Elder in the jump-off. Jim Elder was a member of the 1968 gold-medal jumping team at the Mexico Olympics and a well-respected equestrian in the horse community. It was an incredible thrill for me to give him a run for his money. Jim Day recognized my success with Spot Check and decided to change the horse's name to JC Superstar after the famous musical.

Jim Elder was also impressed by Spot Check, so he came to the farm to ride him. High-end riders were always looking for talented individuals to add to their show jumping line. Jimmy Day priced the horse at ten thousand. Elder, looking for a deal, turned him down.

Jim Day decided to take over the reins of JC Superstar. I always say that I trained the horse Western, but Jim Day rode the horse English. This horse was a sensitive ride and became confused with the rider change. Jim Day and Superstar did not get along. It was not long before Jimmy gave the horse back to me; his name was changed back to Spot Check, and he was moved out into the shed row. I had ridden so many horses by this point that I could adjust to Spot Check's sensitivity. Around the same time all this was happening, a lady showed up to try Spot Check. Jim Day asked for $3500.00, but she did not take him, so I was happy to continue with his training.

Jimmy Day's wife, Dinny, had grown up with horses and had learned to ride. She saw the potential in me and Spot Check. She said, "Hugh, you should buy that horse. You can ride him." I immediately went to the bank and borrowed the money. I called Jimmy, who was competing at the Buffalo, New York, show and told him I wanted to buy Spot Check. He said he had done the math, and the price was now $4500.00. When I told Dinny what Jimmy had said, she stated, "You need to buy that horse." Without hesitation, she wrote me a cheque for the additional $1000.00. She said, "Hugh, you can pay me back when you get the money." Thankful for the support, I called Jimmy back and informed him I had the money. I now owned my first showjumper, Spot Check, and he was talented.

In 1972 I took over managing Sam-Son Farm's boarder barn. Spot Check and I competed at all the local shows: Hamilton Hunt, Aurora, Bolton, London, and Sam-Son Farm's Class "A" Hunter Jumper Show. Spot Check was doing very well, and we had moved up to the Preliminary jumper division. In 1973, I rode Spot Check in the Sutton show near Lake Simcoe, Ontario. I took a chance and entered him in the Modified Grand Prix at 1.35 metres, and we won. I was very excited about what this horse could do. He was careful when he went over the jumps; he didn't want to knock anything down. We were always in the ribbons and earning money.

Three weeks later, at the CNE (Canadian National Exhibition, Toronto), I entered Spot Check in his first Grand Prix at 1.45 metres. The class was a ten-thousand-dollar Rothman's Grand Prix. There were three clears (no knockdowns or refusals) in the first round. The three riders were Torchy Miller, who later became Team Canada's chef d'equipe; up-and-coming star Kelly Hall Holland; and myself. I was the last horse to go and knew what Spot Check and I had to do. We went clear with the fastest time, winning our first gold medal.

The Canadian Equestrian Team approached me about going to Washington for experience, and it was an easy sell. Spot Check and I showed up at the Washington International Horse Show. My team members were Jimmy Day, John Simpson, Ian Millar and Liz Ashton. Would you believe someone put sawdust in the ring for footing and spray-painted it green so it would look like grass? In the first Junior Jumper class, four of the first ten horse-and-rider combinations fell due to the slippery conditions. A riders' meeting was called. The show committee had chosen to cancel some classes to bring in new footing. One of those classes was my first class. I said, "I came all the way from Canada for experience. I thought I was having four classes and I'm not happy with three classes." I was new on the show jumping scene. I'm sure everyone was thinking, *Who is this guy?* Joe Darby stood up and said, "You go back to Canada and do some schooling shows." Then Francis Rowe, the American coach, stood up and said, "In all fairness, this is the Washington International. You should already have your horse schooled and have done your homework, so you're ready to compete." I didn't react, but I also didn't back down, and the class was eventually held. There were two clears: me, and Rodney Jenkins of the United States, who was known as the king of show jumping. Rodney was riding a big roan horse by the name of "Wow" and he beat me in the jump-off.

The next class was a "Hit and Hurry" speed class, and I jumped one more jump than anyone else for the win. As I was coming out of the ring with my blue ribbon, Frances Rowe met me at the in gate and said, "Hugh, I take it all back. You belong here." I said, "Frances, it's all my fault. I said I was coming here for the experience, and I should have been more specific. It was the experience of winning." She laughed, and after that, we became great friends. Spot Check and I came away with a first, second, third and fourth. Those placings earned us Reserve Champion behind Rodney Jenkins, who was the champion.

I came home to the Royal Winter Fair in Toronto, and won the Open Jumper Championship. Spot Check was fit with many ribbons and earnings to prove his ability. Jean Mathers, a businessman in Quebec, came up to me and said, "I always buy the Open Jumper champion at the Royal." Jean bought these horses for his son Jean-Guy Mathers to ride and show. It was a hard decision to sell this wonderful horse but the sale of this horse financed my further endeavours. Unfortunately, it was business.

Hugh Graham's Accomplishments

Hugh Graham has competed on many horses in many cities. He has been an Olympian twice; he competed in four World Cup finals and rode on three teams at the Pan American Games. Hugh rode thirty-nine different horses to Grand Prix wins. He has ridden in twenty-three Nations Cups and competed at the 1990 World Equestrian Games. Twice he was named Equestrian of the Year.

In 1990, Hugh Graham met Seymour and Gloria Epstein. They put their heads together and decided to start King Ridge Stables. Hugh actively participated in breeding, riding and training 200 sports horses. It was not long before King Ridge became the leading jumper stable. On February 6, 2012, Equine Canada named King Ridge Stable the winner of the inaugural Canadian Breeder of the Year award.

Hugh's father-in-law, Morgan Firestone, asked him if he would manage his Thoroughbred racing stable. Hugh said no at first. He was too busy with his other endeavours. Morgan's dream was to win the Queen's Plate. Morgan told Hugh that he didn't have to come to work, he just needed to call the shots. The problem was that calling the shots and making the shots were two different things. Hugh had to get hands-on if he was to be successful, so he started getting up early to ride the Thoroughbreds and watch how they were trained. A horse called Mike Fox was showing incredible promise but was having problems. Hugh took over riding and training of this difficult race horse. The following year, Mike Fox returned to racing, and in June of 2007, Mike Fox won the Queen's Plate while being ridden by the first woman jockey, Emma Jayne Wilson. Hugh stated, "This was the biggest accomplishment in my life." He felt that the anticipation and resulting success of Mike Fox gave the ailing Morgan Firestone an extra year of quality life. Morgan had his dream realized.

In November of 2016, Hugh Graham was inducted into the Equine Canada Show Jumping Hall of Fame.

The award was fittingly presented by Seymour and Gloria Epstein.

Currently Hugh resides in Ocala, Florida, for the winter, then returns to Ontario for the summer. In 2021, Hugh broke his femur one day before he was to return to Ontario. The doctors in Florida decided that the best fix for the femur was to do a total hip replacement. With Hugh's prognosis being excellent, he was told he could be riding in six weeks. Two months later, Hugh entered a Grand Prix, won it, and then won another Grand Prix the following week.

In listing Hugh's accomplishments, we cannot forget to mention his talented horse, Spot Check, a horse who was a sensitive ride requiring a special rider. This horse jumped his heart out for Hugh, kick-starting his show jumping career. Says Hugh, "Spot Check was my first horse, and he was remarkable. My mother never forgave me for selling him. He was such a big part of my life and was very special to me. People have attractions in life; mine is horses."

During our discussions about this story, Hugh said he was thinking of writing a book featuring his horse career, called "Born to Ride." I am sure, when it is completed, it will be a great read from one of Canada's finest horsemen.

The Once-in-a-Lifetime Horse

Fritz & Ingrid Holtz and Marcus

I have known Fritz and Ingrid for quite some time. We competed together and enjoyed each other's company. They are a talented couple in many ways and I can say they know a good horse when they see one. I cannot express how many horses have passed through their hands; only a handful did not pan out as expected.

I love Fritz's story of arriving in Germany to pick out young Holsteiner horses for importing to Canada. Holsteiners were initially bred in a region of Germany called Holstein. Fritz's face would become stern and his voice heightened when he talked about his horse-buying experience. "Germans will bring you out all of their inferior colts, thinking that you are Canadian and would not know any better," he told me. Fritz would watch them run around in the arena, then tell them in German to stop showing him their cast-offs and start bringing out the good horses. From those, he chose the ones he would have the veterinarian inspect and X-ray them for purchase.

When I visited Fritz and Ingrid, they would speak highly of the horses they were presently training and showing. They would reminisce about the great horses they had in the past, but one name kept coming up repeatedly: Marcus. Fritz's eyes sparkled and his voice elevated with excitement when he recalled his time with this great horse. "I never had one like him in the past, and I probably will never find another one like him in the future," Fritz would lament.

Ingrid and Fritz had a comfortable lifestyle. Fritz was an engineer but finally decided to retire to participate in his horse hobby full-time. Ingrid came from Swiss German equestrians who competed at high levels in show jumping. Fritz says, "What I know about horses I learned from my wife."

Husband and wife travelled widely through North America to follow the horse shows and compete. Travelling and competing taught them what to look for in an athletic, well-built horse. It is always a gamble when you buy a young prospect. The horse could be a winner or a loser.

In their travels, Fritz and Ingrid met a retired jeweller named Franz Beck. Franz was a good horseman who also imported horses from Germany. It was through Franz that Fritz first met Marcus.

Franz brought out his sixteen-hands-one-inch, leggy three-year-old, sired by Waterman, a Dutch Thoroughbred stallion, and a warmblood mare. Marcus floated across the ground in a spectacular trot, which immediately took

Fritz's and Ingrid's breath away. They looked at each other and instantly knew that they were looking at something exceptional. Franz knew what he had and priced him accordingly. Marcus was expensive compared to other horses. Franz commented that Shannon Oldham, a well-known dressage rider, had put the bridle and saddle on Marcus for the first time and was thrown off, breaking her arm. Marcus had an attitude. What to do? Did they take a chance on this unproven youngster? They were not discouraged and decided to go with their gut. Marcus would be theirs not to keep but to train and sell.

Fritz and Ingrid took nine horses from Canada and headed to the United States. The group of nine was kept in two stables where they were poorly cared for. In hindsight, they wish they would have stayed with the horses and shown them personally to prospective buyers. They paid professionals at the stable to ride and market the horses. It was a disaster. One of their horses carried five different riders on his back in one day and became lame. Another horse flipped over a jump and injured his back. Marcus was young and inexperienced, and it showed. Lucky for Fritz and Ingrid, no one wanted him, so he returned with them.

Ingrid started to work diligently with Marcus. Every day he improved and started to like his lessons, especially jumping. This horse was clever and tidy with his legs. He did not want to hit the jumps, which was fantastic. He did everything he could to jump clean, plus he had the athleticism to do it.

It was time to leave the comfort of home and school at a nearby cross-country field. Ingrid was anxious to see how brave Marcus would be. What they learned that day was that Marcus had the complete package. He was brave, beautiful to look at, athletic and a fabulous mover.

Fritz learned to be a competent competitor and could see that this horse had the potential to be an Olympic hopeful. Fritz was approaching fifty years old and was in the best shape of his life. He exercised frequently, even running up and down the stairs in hotels. It was time he took Marcus and started competing with him.

Marcus was too good to start at the green level, so they moved him up to Training for his first time out. He kept his cool under pressure in the show ring. He flowed through the dressage phase and was consistent on the cross-country course, jumping clean on the final day. Marcus easily won his first competition.

This was a good start, but both needed to keep up with the progress. Jack Le Goff was a French equestrian who came to coach the American team. He was world-renowned for being a great coach. Jack's famous quote was, "Training is like a religion . . . you have to BELIEVE!" Fortunately for Fritz and Marcus, Jack was in Canada teaching a clinic. Jack singled out Marcus many times to show the rest how it was done. Jack recognized right away that this was an exceptional horse. In this horse, Fritz could believe, but his age was against him. He soldiered on and was enjoying the training process just the same.

Dressage trains the horse to be aware of the aids given by the rider. Three-Day Event horses are not known for doing well in the Dressage test. They are fit to gallop and run and now are expected to be attentive and controlled. Marcus loved to train and perform dressage. His remarkable talent was to float across the riding arena in an extended trot. He often received top marks for that movement.

Marcus took his responsiveness to Fritz's aids into the jump ring. One of Fritz's training techniques was to set up a high chair in the riding arena, with two poles from the chair to the ground in the shape of a "V." The objective was to jump the high chair, which is narrow. Marcus was an honest horse with no thought to refuse or jump to the side. He would repeatedly jump over the high chair without a waver, even without the poles.

Ingrid and Fritz competed against each other at the 1988 Western Canadian Championships in Lloydminster, Saskatchewan. Ingrid was riding her seasoned horse, Merlin, and Fritz and Marcus were poised to give his wife a run for her money. Ingrid loved to tease her husband by saying that Marcus was more brilliant than Fritz. He agreed. If any mistakes were made, it would be his fault, not Marcus's. After the dressage phase, the husband-and-wife team placed first and second. The cross-country phase was a breeze for Merlin. He ran on time with no penalties.

Marcus was always on the muscle, which meant he was strong in the rider's hand. Fritz was galloping to the water jump, with his eyes straight ahead. Marcus jumped big and bold, coming face to face with the prevailing vertical. Fritz felt they were too close and sensed impending disaster, but Marcus did not hesitate. Fritz jumped off. He thought it was better to plan your contact with the ground than to have the horse flip and land on top of you. Amazingly enough, Marcus cleared the vertical and then looked back at Fritz to say, "What are you doing down there?" Fritz could have kicked himself for doubting his horse. He could have won the event if he had stayed on. Adonis was unscathed and jumped faultlessly on the last day. The only injury was Fritz's pride.

In 1989, the Holtzes attended the Western Canadian Games in Winnipeg, Manitoba. The horses flew to Winnipeg, and unfortunately, some arrived with shipping fever. Marcus received veterinary care; he was ready for the competition. Ingrid was first after Dressage, with Marcus second. The cross-country course was formidable, with one jump called a Trakehner consisting of a large, broad ditch, followed by a vertical. The trench was large enough for a horse to run through if the rider chose to do so. The problem with running through the ditch was that it took up valuable seconds, and you would have time penalties. The fastest route was to jump over the ditch and vertical. Ingrid chose to ride through while an Albertan, Kyle Carter, jumped over. Fritz and Marcus were on course. Fritz thought of Jack Le Goff's words, "You have to believe!" Fritz did believe, accepted the challenge and rode confidently straight to it. Marcus, who did not know this jump was a problem, cleared it easily. The pair jumped fault-free the third day and won the competition, with Ingrid second.

Fritz and Marcus checked off the competitions, running faster, jumping better with their eyes on the Olympics. Their first American competition was in North Bend, Washington state. It was usual to arrive one to two days ahead so the horses could see the grounds and get their bearings. The riders took this time to acquire their show package consisting of their number and ride times. The weather was good, so it was a pleasant drive to Washington. Everyone on team Holtz was relaxed as they entered the grounds. Fritz immediately noticed the riders were dressed in their show clothes. Something was wrong, "What is going on here?" Fritz called to a passerby. It was confirmed that this was the first day of the competition. Ingrid could not believe they had made such an error.

They immediately divided up duties. Fritz ran to pick up his show package while Ingrid and their daughter saddled up Marcus. Your test time was written in stone, and missing your assigned time could mean elimination. The downhill spiral of events escalated, as someone forgot to pack the dressage saddle. Ingrid frantically asked their show neighbours if they could borrow one. Usually, the fit was important, but any saddle would do under the circumstances. Fritz returned and scrambled to get dressed. He looked for a tie but could not find one. Again, the neighbour came through with a replacement. Their number was being called, so Fritz and Marcus trotted over to the dressage ring—no time for warm-up, just trot down the centre line and salute. Marcus's eyes were wide with excitement; he was obedient and animated as he demonstrated his lengthened stride. The crowd was in awe as Marcus hyperextended his way across the diagonal, earning him a ten and top spot in the placings. This day's mistake made Marcus even more spectacular. Marcus could keep his mind intact and get the job done despite adversity.

The path to the Olympics was in reach, but Fritz knew he did not have advanced international experience. The horse and rider teams were required to attend qualifying competitions. There were significant costs involved in entry fees, vetting, coaching, stabling and transportation of the horse with no guarantee that you would be selected. Jack Le Goff and others discouraged Fritz from riding as his age and lack of experience was against him. If Marcus was to have a chance, he deserved a younger, more experienced rider.

Fritz looked at his one-of-a-kind horse and decided he would not stand in the way of Marcus's He decided to sell him, not to just anyone but to someone who could take him all the way. Unfortunately, no one in Canada wanted to pay the fifty thousand price tag. During those years, horses were not syndicated in Canada. Jack Le Goff stated that Marcus was the best horse in North America. It was Jack who contacted the US Eventing Association, which included Michael Friedlander, a financial supporter of the great rider Mike Plumb. Michael came to see Marcus and jumped at the chance to buy him for Plumb.

Marcus was talented but inexperienced at the top international level. Mike Plumb knew there was work ahead of them. It takes time for a rider and horse to develop a bond built on trust and understanding. No two riders are the same. The leg, seat and hand aids may feel different to the horse.

Michael and Marcus arrive at Fair Hill, Maryland. The competition was challenging for the pair. Mike had to focus on serious training for the next six months. Corrections were made, and the team came in second at the Checkmate International Competition in Feversham, Ontario. Mike was recorded to have said, "He's a lot easier to ride. I found a way to control Marcus without insulting him." The win assured them a spot on the shortlist for the Olympics in Barcelona.

Dressage Day in Barcelona was a proud day for Michael Plumb, Marcus and Fritz Holtz. Fritz had kept in touch with Mike's progress throughout the preparation journey. This Dressage Day did not disappoint as Marcus performed to an impressive eighth spot with 49.60 penalty points. Three-Day Events are scored in penalty points, and this was a competitive standing.

The next day was Cross-Country; the track was slippery. There had been horses and riders who fell on the course. The jumps were big, wide and tricky. As Fritz watched on closed-circuit television, he saw Mike coming into a multiple jump combination and feared they did not have enough speed. It is critical to have the correct impulsion or power. Marcus gave it his all, but he could not make it. His hind leg hung up on the jump, and Mike came off. He quickly remounted, but the pair had lost valuable time putting them out of the medals. Mike declared later that his ride could have been better. All great riders review what went wrong to improve their future performances.

Fritz reminisced about the disappointment of not riding Marcus at the Olympics. The mishap at the famous event did not diminish how exceptional this horse was to all who worked with him. Fritz to this day is visibly moved when he talks about Marcus; arriving at the horse show late, then experiencing a magical ride that only dreams are made of.

"I have spent the rest of my life looking for a horse with the same talent and mind as Marcus. You only get a horse like him once in a lifetime!" he says.

Marcus is now retired and in the care of a lovely lady who adores him. He gets to live the rest of his days in green pastures with lots of love and attention. A fitting life for such a wonderful horse.

Police Service Horse
Sgt. Fred Rasmussen and Warden
(with a special tribute to Robin Hahn)

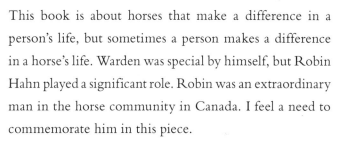

This book is about horses that make a difference in a person's life, but sometimes a person makes a difference in a horse's life. Warden was special by himself, but Robin Hahn played a significant role. Robin was an extraordinary man in the horse community in Canada. I feel a need to commemorate him in this piece.

Robin Hahn was a name that I had known from my teenage years. I made a habit of studying all of the top equestrians. My interest was Canada's jumping team, not Three-Day Eventing, so it was many years before my path would cross with Robin's.

I was riding an Appaloosa named Eekie (his show name was Ezekiel), who had so much talent that he would have excelled at whatever discipline he was asked to do. Linda Ramsay, a coach and rider, talked me over my first cross-country jump on arriving in Kelowna, BC. I was convinced that all Three-Day -Event riders had a death wish or were at least out of their cotton-picking minds to be running and jumping over solid obstacles. You know, the kind of jumps that if you make a mistake and hit them, you fall down—the jump does not! By this time, I was an older rider and should have known better, but Linda talked me into going to Robin Hahn's Longhouse Competition with Eekie.

I hadn't even watched a Three-Day Event, let alone competed in one, but I conceded to go. As it turned out, I was successful and subsequentially hooked. Fast forward a few years, and I was now at Nick Holmes-Smith's competition site.

The directors of Horse Trials BC felt that there needed to be an intermediate step for Event riders to practice the Olympic format. With the Olympic level competitions, the first day was the dressage test; the next day was the endurance phase, which included phase "A" roads and tracks, phase "B" steeplechase, phase "C" roads and tracks, and phase "D" galloping cross-country. If your horse passed the vet check on the third day, you got to jump a course in an arena

. To legally do this format at the Training Level, the directors decided to run it as a clinic, but it would be scored like a competition. This is where I had my first taste of what kind of man Mr. Robin Hahn was.

The Training Clinic competitors met at the steeplechase field a day before the competition started. Robin Hahn was our clinician for the weekend, and he was going to talk us through the expectations for steeplechase, vet checks, roads and tracks, and what would take place in the ten-minute vet box before we galloped off for cross-country.

I remember sitting on my capable Appaloosa, shaking in my leather boots, as we looked at the steeplechase fences. In his deep, quiet, calm voice, Robin took his time to explain in detail, step by step, what would happen when we arrived at the steeplechase field on competition day. The steeplechase fences looked huge. They had cedar boughs sticking out the top, which the horses were supposed to brush through. One by one, he asked us to practice our first jump. What impressed me about Robin was that he always had a good thing to say about each rider and horse. He encouraged us and instilled trust in our own abilities. Robin's heart was totally in what he was doing. We all left the session prepared for what lay ahead of us.

We had several meetings with Robin during the weekend, as he walked us through how to present our horses to the vets, what to wear, and how the ten-minute vet box would work. On competition day, I arrived in the vet box to find Robin there waiting for me as my horse was taken by the grooms to wash, show to the vet and re-saddle for the cross-country. Robin gave me an orange juice and we sat down. He talked, as I visualized every single jump that I was about to execute in the order of go. He gave practical advice: what jumps were jumping well and which ones to be careful of. The experience in his voice gave me confidence, and his soothing tone quieted my nerves. I won that competition, which was partly due to my fabulous horse Eekie, but what made the difference was the excellent coaching of Robin Hahn.

When Robin talked about his riding career, you could see a tear in his eye and hear the pride in his voice as he gave the account of his past and present riding endeavours. Robin carried on riding after surviving a heart attack. He passed away at age eighty-eight in 2021.

Sgt. Fred Rasmussen, RCMP:

This story starts on the banks of Battle Creek in the Cypress Hills of southern Saskatchewan, which in 1875 was known as the North West Territories. Fort Walsh was built by Inspector James Morrow Walsh, plus the "F" Troop of the Northwest Mounted Police.

This unusual landscape consists of pine forests and rolling plateaus, 600 metres above the surrounding prairies. The valley is rich in nature's beauty, where the hills have flat-top and bench land reaching as far as the eye can see. Fort Walsh and the surrounding hills encase the fascinating history of the settling of the Canadian West.

In the spring of 1960, I went on my annual three-month transfer to Fort Walsh Remount Station with the stallions. I came earlier than usual since the ranch foreman at the Fort was commencing sick leave following a severe operation. This was a hectic time of year as we had thirty-five broodmares, nearly all in foal, which required special attention and a watchful eye. The mares were of mixed breed, while the stallions were Thoroughbred. The objective of this breeding program was to add size, strength and the recognizable black colour to the progeny.

The Detachment operated on an open-range program where the mares foaled outdoors in the pastures surrounding the Fort. Early each morning, we would call the mares, summoning them to the feeding grounds near the Fort. With the sun rising in the distance, sending its fingers of light over the land, it was always a source of pleasure to see the herd, some with foals afoot, cresting over the hilltop. As the group headed for the feeding boxes, anticipation was in the air. After the horses settled down to eat, we visually inspected each mare and foal. This ritual was carried out every morning, and again just before the sun nestled behind the hills.

As I counted the horses early one morning, it became apparent that one mare was missing. It was Regimental Number 15, "Fluff," one of our oldest broodmares. I walked to the nearest hilltop to beckon her. There was no response—just silence. I returned to the stables and tacked up one of the saddle horses to go and search. I examined every coulee and hilltop until I finally spotted a long-legged chestnut foal, standing and nuzzling his mother, who was lying lifeless on the ground. I instantly knew I had found my missing mare. This sight gave me such an overwhelming feeling of sadness, not only for the foal who would probably not survive but because we had lost one of our best broodmares. Fluff had given us so many high-quality foals over the years.

I realized I was mounted on Fluff's first foal, a mare named Gem. On the ground, healthy and lively, obviously would be her last baby, a colt. On closer inspection, there were no signs that the mare had been on her feet since delivering, and it was doubtful whether the foal had any of the mother's milk. The first milk is called colostrum, and the foal needs to receive this. The first milk is full of antibodies to fight infection.

I returned to the ranch for help. With the use of a Clydesdale mare named Kit and her foal, we managed to get the newborn to follow us back to the stable. It was heartbreaking to see the little fellow not wanting to leave his mother nor the place where he was born.

In those early years, there was no powdered milk replacement for foals. Mare's milk is structured to a foal's particular needs. Cow and goat's milk were not suitable as they would produce diarrhea. I wanted to save this fine-looking colt, the last foal from our now deceased exceptional mare and number-one stallion, Faux Pas. I needed to develop a solution, and it had to be fast. We needed mare's milk, and I knew where to find it.

Fort Walsh owned two Clydesdale mares who had recently given birth. We began the time-consuming task of bringing them, one at a time, to feed the colt. The mares gave us enough milk for some bottles during the day, and one for the 2:00 a.m. feeding. A staff member would awaken to check all the broodmares and, at the same time, heat a bottle to feed the foal. We even tried to see if one of the mares would accept the orphan. The one mare, Kit, the Clydesdale, knew that she had not given birth to twins and therefore had limited tolerance for the adopted sibling. Bess plainly said no. We hoped to give the little fellow some "horsey mom" time by introducing the mares into the equation.

During the day, we started to keep "Sonny" (a name we chose) in the Fort's enclosure, which had plenty of room for him to roam around, plus it allowed us to keep a close eye on his input and output. My four-year-old daughter and the dogs became his daily playmates. It wasn't long before the lanky youngster had become part of our family. It was so cute and amusing to see my daughter, Kathie, with her long blond pigtails, leading the big Clydesdale mare around with the two foals following along. It wasn't long before Sonny had equated the slamming of the screen door with feeding time. There was no need to call him— once he heard the sound of the door, he came cantering over for his meal.

It was a good day when a neighbour announced that he had a range mare who had lost her foal and we were welcome to use her for Sonny. The mare was not well broke, so it took some doing to get her over to the Fort. After putting our heads together on how to unite the two, we ended up skinning the dead foal and putting it on Sonny's back so that the surrogate mom would accept him as her own. The mare sniffed the pelt and seemed to get excited that her dead foal had made a miraculous recovery. Our plan worked, and Sonny had a mom. She was a dedicated mother to the colt, and there was no doubt she was his salvation. Sonny became strong enough to join the herd. When my daughter came to visit, the foal would recognize her and came running over to play and visit. The somewhat untamed mare would stand a safe distance away whinnying, very anxious to know what was happening with her offspring. She didn't understand the bond we had with this youngster.

As the summer progressed, the foal was given Regimental Number 440 and the name "Warden." I did not see him again until the following spring when I returned with the stallions for another breeding season. He was a very handsome yearling, and it was rewarding to have successfully saved such a fine specimen.

As a two-year-old, Warden was developing as he should. He was the tallest of the two-year-olds, but a little out of place. Warden was a single chestnut amongst a sea of black offspring the RCMP are known for. At the age of three, he did not join the others to be sent to the Regina riding school. Warden was instead designated to become a ranch horse, at least for now.

Over the years, I had worked with many of Fluff's offspring. They all shared the common thread of being "cold backed," which means they did not take kindly to anything on their backs and would let you know about it. On this issue, Warden was true to his genetics. I was an experienced horse person and knew that I could probably manage the problem with time. If not, I might have found a candidate for the Calgary Stampede Bucking Horse class. At the beginning of training, he would react with severe bucking when I put the saddle on, which later, with more patience, would lessen to crow-hopping. It was only then that I endeavoured to get on him. I rode him nearly every day that season and considered him a great saddle horse, even though his cold back did not completely disappear.

In February of 1964, the commanding officer of Depot Division and Fort Walsh requested one of the instructors from the Equitation staff to be his driver for the annual inspection of the Remount Detachment. This was the name given to the horses that would go to Regina to be trained for the Musical Ride. The officer brought up the subject of Warden. He had received a request from the staff at the Fort to consider selling him, since he was the wrong colour for the ride and not suitable as a saddle horse for the ranch. I could not blame them for feeling that way. Warden was seventeen hands high, a young Thoroughbred that could be described as high strung, or at least strung to send his riders high. I tried to stay neutral on this matter, relating the story of his shaky beginning and stating he was undoubtedly out of the best stock on the ranch.

It was fall, so Warden was turned out on the range with the cattle and mares. One week before the cattle round-up, the police horses would be located and herded home to the Fort for the winter. The ranch foreman told a ranch hand to throw his saddle on the truck. It made good sense for them to catch Warden and use him to herd the mares home. They located the mares, saw Warden, bridled him, and with some reluctance, he was saddled. The ranch foreman was unaware of impending doom when he swung his leg over the horse. Warden went airborne, and the rider went flying—high, wide and handsome, in cowboy terms. It took some time to catch Warden and even longer to unsaddle him, which resulted in the ranch staff never riding him again.

Warden was staying put for now. I returned to the Fort the following year with the stallions. Needless to say, I was very cautious when I started to ride him. I have never claimed to be a bronco rider, nor have I ever desired to become one. Each day I got a little further with retraining him and started to ride a greater distance from the Fort. After a couple of weeks, things were going well and seemed to be back to normal. Then came an experience I will never forget.

We were following a relatively high ridge to my right, where there was a view of Fort Walsh, situated on the banks of Battle Creek. To my left, the bench land rose to the horizon, with coulees and hills in between. I guided Warden to a decline from the ridge, and when we crested and took a few steps downward, all hell broke loose. Whether the saddle slipped forward and put pressure on his shoulder where a wound had been, or whether it was the ever-present cold-back reaction, I will never know. However, I can assure you it was not a pleasant experience having a seventeen-hand Thoroughbred going into a bucking spree down a steep hill with plenty of rocks. coupled with lots of elevation. The earliest I could hit the ground from where I was flying was twenty to thirty feet, amongst the stones and cacti. I will never know how I did not break any bones, but I had plenty of bruises. Sitting amongst the rocks and debris, I muttered to myself, "Why did I try so hard to save you?" Warden made it to the bottom and started grazing, very unconcerned over what had just happened. I bravely mounted him and rode him back to the ranch. I couldn't let him get away with this debauchery, so I solicited the help of our ranch foreman. I asked him to ride his horse, Lola, and I snubbed Warden solidly with a lead shank to the horn of Lola's saddle. We made an exercise of riding up and down hills using Lola to teach Warden another way to overcome terrain changes. I continued to ride him daily for the duration of my summer stay at the Fort. Each time there was a downhill descent, it took all the training I possessed not to tense up, but remain calm and relaxed, so as not to give Warden an excuse to explode.

After my return to the riding school in Regina, I was called to the riding master's office, who wanted to know about the chestnut horse at the ranch and if he would be suitable as a troop horse for officer training at the riding school. I could only answer that he could be terribly tense at times and did not like anyone bumping on him when descending downhills. The riding master's response was, "I don't see too many hills around Regina." Warden was transferred to Regina, where he fit well into the riding program.

Ridden by Constable Coldham, Warden took part in the last "pass-out" ceremony at the Depot Division troop. This historical event in 1966 occurred at the RCMP Police Barracks in Regina following eighty-four years of equestrian training. Equestrian training stopped being mandatory for all recruits. Since then, only members assigned to the Musical Ride have received this training. The program would be terminated. By the end of that summer, there would be a transfer of staff, instructors and many horses to the "N" Division, Ottawa, which would involve a sale of horses not being transferred.

It was a heart-rending experience to see these horses I had witnessed being born, helped to train and that had been used as mounts for troops now scattered to the four winds. I hoped each horse found a kind hand to guide them. An owner to use them with care and consideration as the other RCMP officers and I had done over the past years.

As the horses were being dispersed out of Regina, and still having a sweet spot for Warden whom I had rescued and trained, I phoned an equestrian friend in Belle Plaine, Saskatchewan. Robin Hahn was an up-and-coming star of Three-Day Eventing, who would later become captain of the Canadian Three-Day Team. I filled him in on the details concerning Warden and suggested he come to see him. Upon looking over this fine, quality horse and instantly liked him, Robin purchased the tall chestnut for $525.00, a steal of a deal for a horse of his breeding.

I saw the pair in March of 1967 when I attended the Regina Spring Horse Show. It is a very prominent event, and there entering the warm-up arena, I saw my friend Robin leading Warden. As Robin mounted his horse, Warden—true to form—showed his resentment by "crow-hoping" for a few minutes while Robin grinned ear to ear. I knew then the right rider had been found for this horse. In this performance, Warden won his first red ribbon in a major show jumping competition, which was only the beginning. There would be many more ribbons and honours yet to come.

Christopher Robin Hahn's Accomplishments
Biography of a Master

1956 – Alternate rider for Stockholm Olympics with his horse Colette; Robin was also the assistant coach and groom for the riders

1967 – Winnipeg Pan American Games on Warden

1968 – Mexico City Olympics, finishing ninth on Taffy

1972 – Munich Olympics on Lord Jim

1976 – Montreal Olympics on Sunrise and Branch County

1982 – World Championships on Strathallan

1988 – 1990 – Shortlisted for the World Championships with Welton John

Coaching Experience:

- Coach for many young riders' teams representing Ontario, Saskatchewan and BC

- Coach for the Jamaican Pan American Championship Team of 1990

- Owner of Longhouse farm in Lumby, BC, where he hosted Three-Day Eventing

- Level III Eventing Coach, helping to create Canada's Coaching Certification Program

The Horse from Hell

Joy Kimler and Golden Boy

I grew up in a small Northern Ontario town named New Liskeard. In the late 1960s, there was no Pony Club, 4-H, or any competent coaches. A handful of people owned horses, but most had no formal training. As a young horsewoman, I was on my own to ride and train my horse.

I believe that people are born with a horse gene, as there were no others in my family who loved horses. My parents told me that "horse" was my first word as a baby, not mommy or daddy. I am sure that was not true, but it made for a good story. I was born in 1954, which was the Chinese year of the horse. My siblings were baffled by my passion. When choosing a topic for a school assignment, I always chose horses. I drew, dreamt about, and read books on horses.

My father, Ed Collier, was the proprietor of Hinds and Collier Men's and Boy's Wear clothing store. As a young person, I thought that we were rich. Looking back, we were probably middle class. I had begged for a horse for years. It was a financial stretch, but my parents sent me to riding school at twelve years old. The stipulation was if I did well at riding school, they would buy me a horse.

Since tidying up my room was an impossible feat, my parents hoped I would not enjoy cleaning stalls or other unpleasant tasks associated with owning a horse. I would not be surprised if my dad paid the riding school teacher, Barbara Lloyd, of Barrie, Ontario, extra money to make the work as hard as possible, hoping that I would come home disillusioned. How wrong they were.

My riding school mount was a large palomino horse by the name of Champ. I loved him. I loved the routine, the smell of manure and the camaraderie of the other girls. I came home even more enthused. Did I mention that my parents sent me to an English riding school with a Western hat and cowboy boots? We weren't aware that there was a difference.

My attitude meant they needed to come clean on their promise to buy me a horse of my own. Knowing nothing about horses, my parents could have used a knowledgeable person to help with the decision. In my hometown, there was no one like that. My dad made a few calls and found a horse for sale. Being young and horse crazy, it didn't matter what horse they showed me—I would love it as long as it had a head and a tail, whinnied and ate hay.

As we drove down the driveway, we could see a beautiful palomino horse. Linda Gannon had Golden Boy decked out in a beautiful Western parade saddle with a fancy fur-trimmed saddle pad. There, standing before me, was a sixteen-hand handsome gelding who presented himself regally. I knew right away that this was the horse of my dreams. I don't remember if I even sat on his back, checked to see if he was sound or asked any questions. My dad, at my pleading, paid $275.00 for the horse, bridle and saddle. I had requested an English saddle, which the owners were able to provide. I was too inexperienced to check if the equipment fitted the horse correctly or if the bit on the bridle was suitable. Nothing mattered at that point.

My mother, Anne Collier, did not venture out of the car the first time she came to see Goldie. Mom politely rolled down the window and said, "He is nice, dear," and promptly rolled up the window. This was not going to be a match made in heaven.

Behind the barn at the Gannons' farm was a large flat field I could ride in. Heading back to the stable, I went through a gate and down a lane, turning a sharp right corner past the manure pile to the front of the barn. I did not know that formidable pile and I would become intimately involved. As it turned out, a stainless-steel bit was no match for Goldie's iron-clad mouth. I would ride in the field endlessly, where he would go along with the program for a while and then put his head down and head for the barn at warp speed. I was physically helpless as I hung on to the reins for dear life. He would careen around the corner of the barn, flinging me off into the manure pile like a sack of potatoes thrown into the bed of a truck. I was stubborn like my father, so being Ed Collier's daughter, I was not deterred by this horse I had yearned for so long. The first twelve times I rode him, I fell off twelve times. At least the manure pile was soft, so the only thing that hurt was my pride. My mother, who drove me to and from the farm, threatened to drag me behind the car because I smelled bad.

We had purchased the horse from hell, and either I was going to give up on horses, or I was going to learn to ride. The Gagnons lived down the highway a fair distance, so my parents decided to move Goldie to the McLeans' dairy farm, which was much closer.

The McLeans' two sons, Richard and his brother Donny, rode their Western horses, Lucky and Lightning. My parents hoped I would get some help from them to ride this unruly palomino. Since the boys were Western riders, I was convinced that they could not possibly help me ride English.

If my memory serves me well, I think we paid $25.00 a month for the horses' board. All of that money and more went to repairs on things Goldie had broken or destroyed. Goldie, Thunder and Lucky lived in the calving barn. An electrical box servicing the calving and milking barns was located in Goldie's stall. The breaker box was full of switches and wires. Being sure that no electrician had ever been called to adjust the wiring, Goldie took it upon himself to make the necessary changes. Anything his lips could reach was up for exploration, examination and manipulation. I heard later, after the fact, that the milking equipment in the barn would spontaneously stop working. Lights would be shut off and come back on again. While puzzling over the situation, and being an experienced farmer, Herb McLean traced the problem back to the electrical box in Goldie's stall. Goldie was amusing himself, flicking the switches back and forth. He must have enjoyed the feel of the levers snapping on his tender nose. Herb decided to install a mesh box over the electrical connections. This should foil Goldie's attempts at being a journeyman electrician. The horse analyzed the new situation and repeatedly tried to get his lips inside the tiny wire squares. It was to no avail. The only thing left to do was dismantle the whole darn thing and rip it off the wall. Herb and the boys returned to the calving barn to check on their installation. They saw Goldie huddled in the farthest corner of his stall, away from the array of hanging metal and wires. Goldie's eyes were wide open in dismay, trying to convince everyone he had no idea how a thing like this could have possibly happened! It was back to the drawing board for the McLeans.

Goldie had his own mind, and he thought that rounding up the Holstein cattle seemed like a good idea. During one of his rounding-up exercises, he went through three strands of barbed wire. He was not hurt, except for three pinpricks from the barbs. The cows knew they had been set free and proceeded to run wild all over the farm and surrounding land. Richard and Don saddled up the two Western horses to spend the better part of a day rounding up the cows back into a secure enclosure. I am sure that Goldie would have rounded them up for his own amusement if they had asked. Goldie was never allowed to run with the cows again. His herding days were over.

My riding was improving, and I fell off less frequently. I often had bloody fingers and knees, but nothing was going to deter me. With my sister Betty having newly acquired her driver's licence, she was delegated to be my chauffeur. Betty was outraged that she had to be my driver as a teenager. It was boring. To spice things up, I insisted she ride Goldie. I wanted to share my passion, and it was a chance to see my horse perform from the ground. On this day, Betty seemed to be enjoying a nice ride out in the field. She was cantering along when Goldie saw something that spooked him, or he just wanted to get rid of my sister, so he bolted to the side . . . and Betty took a dive into the pasture.

We all wore glasses in our family, so Betty was on all fours, more concerned about finding her glasses than being hurt. I trundled out to where the mishap occurred, quite amused by the scene. Goldie appeared to join the search with his head to the ground, sniffing and wondering what Betty was doing. Betty was afraid he would mistakenly find her glasses first and crunch them like a potato chip under his large hooves. It took a while, but we did locate her glasses unscathed. My sister made much of the incident, which inspired my parents, after many heated discussions, to buy a small acreage. We could build a barn so that the horse could be at home while our family enjoyed the country life.

My father, God rest his soul, never wanted to be a retail person. He loved to read the horse books I brought home from the library. He cherished the horses, loved his daughter riding, and loved his rum and Coke. I am not sure what order that all came in. Once we moved onto the acreage on Dawson Point Road, he delighted in clearing the land that our house and stable would be built on. He skinned the bark off felled trees to make fence rails for the horse enclosures. When I look back on that experience, I marvel at my father for his dedication and work so that we could have the horses at home.

We had a typical country barn raising. All the neighbours came to help hammer up a three-stall, one-tack-room stable. The hay was stored in the tack room until the barn was completed the following year. Inside the tack room, the electrical box was safe and secure, out of Goldie's reach, with a locking door for extra security.

It was a grand system where the doors to the stalls could be opened, so the horses could go out through a corridor to an enclosure. The riding arena doubled as a turnout paddock. We also had a smaller paddock to the left, another turnout, plus the manure disposal site. It would take some doing to fall off into that manure pile. My father missed his garden and proudly planted one next to the horses' turnout. The wild rabbits made short work of the cabbage while Goldie reached over the fence to munch contentedly on the growing ears of corn. My dad would have to rethink the garden for next year.

Goldie had a friend called Crocket, a Morgan/Quarter Horse cross. My grandpa Shand bought me Crocket as a foal who came from a PMU (pregnant mares' urine) breeder. At a PMU farm, the pregnant mares' urine was collected to extract the estrogen used in birth control pills. The foals were sold off cheap, as they were of no value to the establishment. We were now a two-horse family, and my mother, who was still not very horse-wise, would semi-willingly put the horses out during the day. I would bring them in when I came home from school.

We were sure Goldie had been a locksmith in his previous life. My father skillfully came up with several locking devices to keep Goldie in his stall. None of them worked. We had even discussed a combination lock. It was suggested that I needed to hide the combination so that Goldie would not learn it. When push came to shove—literally—Goldie would ram himself against his stall door and rip the bolts out of the wood. My poor mother would open up the big sliding door at the front of the barn in the morning to be confronted with Goldie's magnificent face and round shining eyes looking back at her. Quickly closing the sliding barn door, she would call me at school. "Goldie is out again," she would lament. "I will come to pick you up." That was the best standing excuse to leave the building . . . I am amazed that I graduated from high school! Goldie was AWOL, and my mother was too afraid to back him up so that he could enter his stall. Not only did I return Goldie to his stall, but I became quite the handyperson, fixing his door until Dad came home from work.

With rum and Coke in hand, dad watched the horses mill around in the outdoor arena that he had built. It brought him peace and joy. I could tell he was proud of his accomplishments. Dad installed an aluminum gate with a very elaborate fastener on this day. You would take the chain and twist it around the spiral-shaped catch, and the gate would be secure. Surly, Goldie would never figure that one out. My father was a methodical man, but he lacked experience in farm duties. While sitting with his cigarette, rum and Coke in hand, he observed Goldie surveying the new gate. Goldie, with his curious, agile muzzle, played with the chain. This problem was going to take more exploration. He directed his attention to the end with the hinges. He grabbed the metal with his teeth and gave it a rattle. Goldie's eyes were full of sparkle and enthusiasm. He had been given a puzzle that needed to be solved. With patience and thought, Goldie lifted the gate and threw it on the ground. Dad had missed one crucial step: He needed to install the bottom bracket facing upward and the upward bracket facing downward, so that a certain street-wise palomino could not remove the gate. I often tried to prove my righteous father wrong in my teenage impudence, but my horse did it in one fell swoop.

We stopped trying to keep him in a fence after that. It was easier to let him out of the front of the barn to roam around the property. Occasionally, he went across the road and herded the neighbour's beef cattle for old times' sake. We would receive a friendly call telling us Goldie was across the street at the Gibsons' farm, and I would head out to collect him.

People fishing at the government dock could see Goldie drinking from the lake. A Good Samaritan would come to the house stating, "Your horse is loose." We would thank them politely and let them know we knew, but there was no point in trying to contain him.

Other issues evolved with Goldie's new freedom. Dad decided it was time to get rid of the old beast of a boat and buy a brand-new Starcraft. He was proud of his new toy, which lived beside the house. Conveniently, we launched the boat into the lake with Dad's Ford Bronco. We spent many hours fishing, eating corned beef sandwiches (my mother called it "bully beef" because there was a picture of a bull on the can) and drinking beer. For a long time, Goldie paid no attention to the boat, so he must have been bored or just noticed the new addition to the property. He smelled the vinyl seats and examined the motor and steering wheel. Apparently, they don't make things the way they used to. Goldie grabbed the vinyl seat back and gave it a mighty yank. The upholstery ripped with no trouble. All you could see when looking at the boat was white foam and large pieces of blue vinyl. Dad was furiously mad that his new toy had been defiled, but he loved that old horse, and he quickly forgave him.

Goldie and I, over the years, came to an agreement on the riding issue. During walk, trot and canter, he became responsive and obedient to my aids. Jumping was another matter. He clearly did not want to jump, and we continued to get eliminated from every jumping competition. One of the biggest jumps we accomplished was not actually part of the stated jump course.

Coming from a small community, it was exciting to compete in another town. Englehart had a horse show, so we loaded up Goldie with great expectations. I was never short on hoping that this would be the competition where I would finish a jump course and not be eliminated. The match was indoors, which was new to both of us. Englehart had taken their hockey arena and filled it with sand. At one end was an observation gallery, and at the other, the two large doors the Zamboni would come through from the outside to clean the ice. I entered through those doors to jump my course. I was pumped with anticipation. The first two jumps came down the near side, facing the doors. One of the spectators standing at the entrance gate was none other than Richard McLean from the dairy farm where we had boarded Goldie. I did my approach circle and cleared the first jump. Goldie felt confident and eager. I was in good form, with my course clearly etched in my mind. The second jump was perfect, and then it happened: Goldie grabbed the bit and saw his chance. We were perfectly aligned for the exit gate with a slight veer to the right. Before Richard knew what was happening, he saw Goldie's hooves clear his shoulder as we exited the Englehart arena in magnificent show jumping style. May the record show that we cleared at least three feet nine inches, which was the most significant jump this horse ever accomplished. One spectator had to change his underwear, and one rider was praising God that she did not die. In a community where family coming home for the holidays was in the classifieds section, my fiasco made front-page news in the local paper. My father could have crawled under a rock and died of embarrassment. It read: "Local retailer's daughter jumps out of the Englehart arena on large palomino horse. Both horse and rider are doing well."

Such as it was for Goldie and me. He had more charisma than a political leader and the brilliance of Einstein. He taught me that riding a horse took more than just sitting there and looking pretty. You had better put on your thinking cap and not be put off by the odd shy-and-run-away tactic. Riding Goldie took hard work and determination. This palomino was a force to be reckoned with. Goldie eventually got chronic obstructive pulmonary disease, better known as Heaves in the horse world. He became frail as the disease progressed. I felt that my dear friend would be deceased every time I went into the barn, so I needed to make the hard call and do what was kind to him. I left for college and asked my parents to do the right thing.

My mother found someone who would come and put Goldie out of his misery. The day he was euthanized, my mother said he went out of the barn with his head held high, more alert than he had been. They loaded him onto the truck, and the deed was done. I know it was the right thing to do in my heart. We all cried in grief, especially my mother, who had learned to tack him up and go for a short ride. Golden Boy was a significant presence demanding our attention with his antics. This beautiful palomino had made hoof prints in all of our hearts.

Goldie was a free spirit who lived life using his own rules. He taught me to ride and not to give up. I learned how to find solutions for challenging, intelligent horses. During my horse career, I did not shy away from tough cases. I am sure that he went to heaven for all the good he did, even though he was the horse from hell. I will never forget him.

My Teacher Dan
Lisa Coulter and Dan

I did not know a Western rider I wanted to use for this book, so I took to the internet for some inspiration. In the Western discipline, there are many facets to choose from: calf roping, gaming, Western pleasure, halter and the list goes on. I wanted someone who has risen to the top of their particular discipline, plus someone I could relate to. Lisa Coulter was the obvious choice. Her story and mine were similar initially, but then she went on to be a director and sit on committees to further her sport. When I received her story about Dan, I knew I had chosen well.

Lisa Coulter:

"I'll be back in a couple hours, Mom," I yelled as I ran outside. I exited quickly, slamming the door to avoid questions about where I was going. It was my personal secret mission.

I picked up my cracked and faded orange skipping rope, and looped it over the handlebars of my red ten-speed bike. My feet pumped up and down as I speeded on my route, taking me around the whole neighbourhood. I passed many closely built houses and empty treed lots, searching for my destination. Ahead was Lions Park, where I screeched to a halt. Dismounting the bike, I walked into the park where I sat, dreaming and waiting. I clung on to that knotted skipping rope, believing that at any moment, I would fling the loop over the neck of a wild horse, gentling him and saying, "You are now mine."

I wasn't nuts, just a typical eight-year-old girl in fourth grade. Cute as a button with freckles and strawberry blond hair. I was tenacious, stubborn, a dreamer and hopelessly horse crazy. I kept my mission secret. I believe that until I wrote this story, no one ever found out. Since wild horses did not show up, I decided it was time to hang up the skipping rope and try a new technique that would possibly bring me better results. I moved on to begging and pleading with my parents to buy me a horse.

My parents knew well enough of my horse craziness. On family trips, we could not pass a trail riding sign on the highways without my relentless pleading to stop. My sister Korri backed me up, as she also loved to ride.

I begged my friends who owned horses to let me ride. I spent my two months away from school searching for and finding anything involving horses. My parents paid for me to attend week-long horse camps. They had some peace and quiet, and I had quality horse time.

After my friend's very naughty pony, Candy, ran off with me, my parents finally agreed to buy me a horse. It was my first 4-H show. Mom and Dad were horrified when I fell and hit my head on a rock. After being unconscious for a short time, I was rushed to the hospital for stitches. Even with this mishap, I still showed that cow of a pony the next day at the fair—stitches, concussion and all. My parents were amazed at my dedication and devotion, feeling I deserved a horse of my own.

I was now ten years old and on a massive search. I combed ads in the newspapers and contacted all the horse people I knew. I hoped to find the absolute right horse that could fit its neck into my old skipping rope. He did not have to be wild; he just had to be mine. The day came when I believed I had found him.

It was immediate love at first sight. The ten-year-old gelding's name was Ray's Dapper Dan (just Dan for short), and he was perfect. He had been trained as a roping horse, which he did until I owned him. He cost my parents $1200.00, and looking back, I realize the sacrifice they made. This horse was a luxury beyond our means. We lived in a modest house in Princeton, just three hours east of Vancouver. My mom, Zandra, was a bank teller and my dad, Marv, was a millwright. Not one other person in my family was a horse person. My parents bought Dan for me, paying his board and other needs for years. Not once did they complain about any of it. My mom and dad hoped this horse would be a good influence on me.

Dan was a beautiful sorrel, sixteen-hand Quarter Horse. His head boasted a star, strip and snip, with two white-coloured hind pasterns. His body was solid and well-built, but the most remarkable thing about Dan was his eyes. Dan's eyes were soft, kind and slow-blinking. Nothing on a horse shows intelligence, gentleness and a calm devoted soul more than large, soulful eyes. I have not found eyes that compare to Dan's to this day.

I wanted and completed everything with Dan that anyone could do on horseback. Dan had only been in a Western saddle, but soon enough, I had the English on him and was heading for jumps. I did not throw away his rodeo skills, as I learned to rope a calf. We entered our local rodeo, where I took home a cheque for my seven-second catch. They call that breakaway roping. Running around three barrels at speed looked fun, so we tried that. We weren't fast but accurate enough not to knock down any barrels; that had to count for something.

The desire to excel at all horse disciplines did not coincide with my skills. I was learning on my own with no local coaches. I would fearlessly compete at the local open shows, watching and learning, trying to copy what others were doing. Dan and I returned home to our makeshift arena, working on mastering what I thought we should know and do. I had cleared an open flat area in a field and put poles along the ground to give us a perimeter. It was primitive, but it would serve us well.

Dan and I went on to many years of wins and successes in the show pen. Our times together were filled with happiness and pure joy. He was my true confidant and my very best friend. Oh, the things I would tell that horse on our long trail rides through the Princeton hills! Dan was a regular favourite at the horse shows, and everyone who met him loved and adored him.

Reminiscing about those times fills my heart with longing for those days with Dan but also with some regret. In my quest for the perfect lead change and ultimate collection, I sometimes ignored my deep love for my horse in pursuit of perfection. I bumped on Dan's mouth and kicked at his sides. I would routinely break down in tears as I cried out in frustration at not getting the super slow jog or expertly executed half pass. Dan would tirelessly stay patient and quiet while I sobbed and sobbed. He knew my tears would end, and eventually, we would calmly carry on. I would gather myself and try again. He would execute the expected collected lope or neatly stepped turn on the haunches with perfect precision and technique. Dan knew the hand and leg aids from previous training. He was patient and did not respond when I asked incorrectly. It took me a while, but I figured out how to ask correctly, and then he would move off, teaching me how it was done. Dan did not pin his ears, swish his tail in disgust, throw his head or kick at my leg. Horses love repetition and constancy. They use that to know what is correct and how to please their riders. It's remarkable and slightly incomprehensible.

I was the type of kid who learned from my mistakes. I would still get the same reward if I did things correctly and wisely, minus the crying sessions! At that very impressionable age, I realized that rough hands, busy legs and lousy horsemanship would get no reward. Until I executed the right cue with the correct leg pressure, held and released with soft hands timed perfectly and applied my seat appropriately, my horse would not give me the much sought-after reward. Through my trust for Dan, I developed a belief in myself. Dan's confidence spilled into me and my tears quickly dissolved. I think all riders will agree that great horses make great riders. What would we be without our willing mounts?

I soon covered the walls in my bedroom with ribbons and plaques. Trophies littered my shelves. I was learning how to win and have confidence. Dan had no problem extending his trot in an English saddle or speeding it up for a barrel run. He would swiftly change gears for a set of pleasure and trail classes.

As the days went by, I discovered Western events suited me more than English. I enjoyed the softness and collection required of a pleasure horse. The obstacles in a trail class posed training situations that spoke to my ever-developing perfectionist personality. I loved riding a Western reining pattern with its precision and exact lead changes in the middle of the circles. All aspects required of the Western horse discipline appealed to me and my desire to ride at a high level. Dan was the first horse I ever performed a sliding stop on (well, a very short sliding stop as I had no idea what slider shoes were). Dan didn't know that we didn't have the equipment or the pedigree to compete at reining, pleasure horse, dressage or jumping. Dan did his job without complaining or hesitation.

Dan and I went to my first big show when I was about thirteen; it was the PNE in Vancouver. It was going to be the most challenging show I had ever been to, with riders from all over BC competing to win. Once we settled into our stalls, I led Dan around to check on the site. It was my first look at the arena where the competition would occur. I stood in the centre, looking up at the high stadium ceiling. Dan looked around, taking it all in stride. I felt dizzy and nauseous by the enormity of it all.

Dan's name will not show up with titles or AQHA accolades by his name, but Dan goes straight to the record book of my heart. I believe he was the most talented and willing horse I have had the good luck and fortune to ride. I have been fortunate to ride some of the most outstanding reining horses in the industry, and I say with all honesty and sincerity that none of these horses had the heart of Dan.

About this time, Dan developed arthritis in his joints. I did not have the resources or knowledge to help the situation as much as I wished. Through all the pain he must have had in those feet, Dan did not give up or stop trying his hardest. I genuinely think he simply loved to do his best, while his heart did not have room for pain. Eventually, I had to stop riding him. In our small town, Dan lived out his years in a pasture. We tried our best to always make Dan's life free of pain and comfort, including spoiling him with love, as we tended to his every need. It soon became apparent that the pain was becoming intolerable, and we could not manage it. The hard decision was made to put Dan to rest.

I will never forget Dan or the lessons he taught me. Horse training has been my life and passion. I have accomplished goals and reached dreams that I did not think were possible. I owe it all to those days in the field with Dan.

Dan taught me the contact of my hands on the reins, the use of my seat in the saddle and the pressure of my legs against his sides. Dan made me the rider I am today through his patience and level-headedness. If Dan could have talked to me, he would have started by slipping his long sorrel neck into my faded old orange skipping rope loop and said, "There, there, Lisa. Stop crying and fussing. Trust the horse sense and talent God has given you, and just ride."

I deeply miss that wonderful horse. My teacher—Dan.

Lisa Coulter's Accomplishments

Throughout her riding career, Lisa excelled in the male-dominated sport of reining:

2003 – Director at Large for Reining Canada

2008 – Joined the Canadian Reining High Performance Committee

Member of the Equine Canada Competition Committee

2009 – Competed on the winning team and was the individual silver medalist at the CR14★ World Equestrian Games

One of two Canadians chosen to compete at the World Reining Masters

The Perfect Horse

Leslie Reid and Seafox

Leslie Reid's riding career started at two years old on her parents' farm. They enrolled her in Pony Club as soon as they could. She was dedicated, moving up the ranks until she passed her Pony Club "A" test in 1975. If you are unfamiliar with a Pony Club "A," it is difficult to pass but worth it as it counted as a credit for high school.

On the other side of the world, in 1982, another champion was being born. A fabulous liver chestnut colt came into the world by the stallion Roemer. Roemer was born in Germany while standing stud in the Netherlands. He was a handsome seventeen-hand chestnut stallion who was multitalented. Roemer competed in jumping, then was imported to the US by Mary Alice Malone in 1985, where he continued being trained as a dressage horse. Roemer excelled to the Grand Prix Dressage Level in three years. Quite remarkable. He was a KWPN stallion, which means he is in the studbook of the Royal Dutch Sport Horse Society, and earned a USDF (United States

Dressage Federation) performance certificate at Grand Prix. It was apparent this new young colt had some impressive heritage.

Kiersten Humphry grabbed Leslie Reid in 1986 to travel abroad to find a jumping horse. Both girls were competitors in jumping, so they had a common interest. They travelled to many stables in Holland, where they found lovely young horses who would make excellent prospects.

Leslie called friends she had made while competing at the World Cup in Belgium the year previous. They suggested a farmer down the road who was rumoured to have a lovely stallion for sale. Kiersten and Leslie turned into the driveway of the hobby farm, looking at pigs and sheep. It was not uncommon for farmers to have a mare that they bred and this farmer bred to the best he could. Leslie and Kiersten were wondering once they arrived where the youngster could be. The property had a very low barn that housed the livestock. The farmer and his son ducked their heads, bending their knees to go into the structure. They returned with a lovely seventeen-hand liver chestnut stallion. When asked if he was backed to ride, the son stated, "Sort of." He had been on him a handful of times. The son hopped on bareback and rode him in what appeared to be the sheep pen. The horse was perfect. He was beautiful, quiet, easy to handle, great conformation. Kirsten bought him, and they all flew back to Langley, BC.

Everything was going great until Kiersten found out she was pregnant. It was a tough decision, but she decided to sell the stallion she called Sea Fox. Leslie and her mother, Edith Thompson, agreed to partner and purchase him. Sea Fox was a successful jumper at the shows for the next two years. At the same time, Leslie was taking dressage lessons and felt this career change would be a good fit for Sea Fox.

Leslie loved that Sea Fox had fluid movement; he was easy to ride and light on his feet. He was intelligent and quiet, just like his father. Sea Fox was a gentleman in every way. He did not offer to bite or kick no matter what, which was strange for a stallion. When he took a treat out of their hands, Sea Fox would grab it with his lips while keeping his teeth closed, making sure he didn't nip the skin. Sea Fox could be feisty. Leslie said, "He bolted a few times in a test—not to be mean, he was just frisky."

Sea Fox's first dressage shows were in the area of Langley, BC. The pair started at the Basic Level and methodically moved up. During his Training Level year, they competed in the Seattle World Cup Qualifier and scored 80%, which in those days was unheard of. The only thing that bothered Sea Fox was the crowd's noise when he received his prize. Leslie learned the trick of putting cotton in his ears to muffle the sound. He was better after that.

The horse and rider pair were seeing success and entered a Talent ID Clinic officiated by Christilot Boylen. Christilot is a well-respected Canadian dressage rider and

Olympian. She looked at Sea Fox and decided he was not a good enough mover to excel to the higher levels. Leslie was not put off and continued training her stallion.

Horsewomen are tough and resourceful. They will go to great lengths to get to competitions. Leslie told me a great story of her adventure to Ontario.

"I set off driving two stallions—one being nine-year-old Sea Fox and one a gelding—to the Pan American Trials in Toronto. The weather was terrible. I spent four days in wind and rain. Previously, I had made arrangements to overnight the horses at a stable in Barrie, Ontario. We arrived at 10:00 p.m., ready for a rest. The lady who owned the farm had forgotten I was coming and said she had no room for my horses. She directed me to a man down the road who she thought had some stalls. I drove into the yard to find out the stalls were goat pens. They would not do.

I pulled out of the goat farm to find my trailer lights weren't working. Not knowing what to do, I found a convenience store. My solution was to buy flashlights and duct-tape them to the trailer. I drove another eight hours until I arrived at the show grounds. Sea Fox came out of the trailer with a kink in his neck that he could not straighten out. That is until he saw the grass nearby."

Leslie and Sea Fox showed well and completed two months of trials. He finished sixth in the standings. Leslie's other horse, Lestat, made the team. Sea Fox was presented for the second time at the ID Clinic, and this time he passed.

If the pair were to advance in their standings, it was necessary to go to the big shows. That meant a plane ride to Europe. Leslie was now thirty-four and admitted she did not know much about flying with a horse, so she ordered a standing stall box to carry Sea Fox on the airplane. She trusted the horse transport company to arrive safely with Leslie's precious cargo and find the relatively small standing box for the plane. She also did not realize that the rest of the airplane horse passengers were mares.

Sea Fox was entertained by his mares, which he now thought were his harem. He travelled well except for the turbulence, which made him nervous and caused him to scramble in his crate. While flying, each horse needed to have a person with them. They are big animals and the last thing the airline needed was a twelve-hundred-pound horse throwing him/herself around. It took everything Leslie could do to calm him and keep him on his feet. The unloading went well until the mares were taken away; he did not like that. Horses are quick to bond with travel companions.

Leslie trained hard in Europe from 1992 to 1996 as a working student. Christilot Boylen and her partner Udo Lang were her coaches. Her goal was always to go to the Olympics. Sea Fox carried Leslie to shows in Liepzig, Stuttgart, and Donaueschingen in Germany, as well as Rotterdam in the Netherlands. They had many top placings and were getting much better as a team. In 1995,

Sea Fox competed in his first Grand Prix in Frankfurt, Germany. They placed third.

It was back to Canada and to The Toronto Royal Winter Fair. It is a prestigious event hosting international rider, who ride show jumpers and hunters. The show includes the Volvo World Cup Dressage Competition. The Volvo event showcased fifteen of the best horses from all over the world. This field of elite horses and riders would probably represent their country at the Olympics the following year. Sea Fox and Leslie had worked hard to be in this group and were elated to win—and yes, they were awarded a Volvo car to drive for a year. This was their best showing to this point.

Next year was the Olympics, and for horses and their riders, it was a busy time going to competitions and training camps. It was a requirement from Dressage Canada that potential team members needed to attend. Tensions were high, and what was best for the horses was always considered.

The Dressage Committee felt they needed to drop the qualifying markdown to 60%, which put Leslie trying out with many horses. At the end of each dressage test, the team is marked for every movement they perform. Usually, the qualifying mark to be considered for the Canadian team is 70%. Christilot said to Leslie that Sea Fox, with all of his experience in Europe, was the only horse in Canada that decidedly had qualified. No other horse had done what Sea Fox had accomplished. Being her first time trying out for the team, Leslie felt it necessary to complete the trials but later wished she had listened to Christilot. It was too much. "I know that now but did not know that then," Leslie said

She arrived at the stables to find Sea Fox clearly in pain. He was lying down, agitated and looking at his stomach. Team vets were called in and, after an examination, decided that he had colic. Colic is stomach upset in horses. Sometimes the horse is plugged up with stool, and infrequently, his stomach or intestines have rotated or telescoped into each other, which calls for surgery. Most colic is not that serious and will pass with medication and time. The next day most horses can be well and continue training or competing. It was up to the team vets whether Sea Fox would be considered for the Olympics.

Leslie stated, "I found out later that he did not have colic. It was ulcers. The vets had no concrete diagnosis at the training camp. He did get better, but it was too late. The vets figured out much later that Sea Fox had mini-episodes that could have been treated. He would have come out of it one hundred per cent. It was a bad situation. It was a sad thing that he did not get to go. He should have gone. The committee picked a lame horse instead of Sea Fox. That horse, in the end, did not go either."

Sea Fox taught Leslie a valuable lesson. Years later, she was asked to attend trials with another of her dressage mounts, the only horse in Canada to get a consistent 70%.

She refused to put her horse through that when he had already proved himself.

It was not Sea Fox's desire to be a Grand Prix horse. Leslie found out later that the stallion Roemer did not produce great Grand Prix horses because they were too quiet, slow and lazy. An interesting piece about Sea Fox was that he was trained to Grand Prix and did the movements for Leslie, but If she put others on him, he wouldn't canter. The student would give the canter aid, and nothing would happen. He didn't like piaffe (trot on the spot); it was not his thing. He was sixteen before he would do it without drama. Leslie said that Sea Fox did not have a great extended trot, but he made up for it with his half pass and his canter work, which was always good. All horses, like people, have movements they do well and have to work hard on the rest.

Leslie said, "I knew nothing of the dressage world—he took me up the levels to Grand Prix. Sea Fox competed up to seventeen years old. I didn't want to push him up to a level where he would struggle. I wanted him to go out on top." Sea Fox taught a young rider, Angela Martin, until the age of twenty, when he officially retired.

Leslie finished up our interview with this: "I have had many horses to train before him and after him. I now know how special he was, both in his character and to have been competitive in the international circle. Sea Fox sired several lovely horses that people enjoyed. He remained 150% sound during his whole career until the end. No one knew my horse was blind in one eye. I bought him with a small cataract that was diagnosed when he was eight years old. It never bothered him. He was generous, kind and beautiful. One of a kind. Sea Fox passed away in 2011 at twenty-nine years old."

Udo Lang, Christilot Boylen's partner, said. "Sea Fox was absolutely the perfect horse— conformation, structure, character, the way he could move, his technique."

Leslie Reid remarked, "He was the perfect horse— handsome, honest, and the gentlest stallion one could ever have."

Leslie Reid's Accomplishments

1996 - First place on Sea Fox at the Volvo World Cup Dressage League Final at the Toronto Royal Winter Fair

1999 - Competed in the Pan American games riding Gokker Z

2003 - Individual Gold Pan American Games in Santo Domingo, Dominican Republic, plus Team Silver riding Mark

2004 - Athens Olympics riding Mark

2005 - Dressage World Cup Final riding Mark

2008 - Beijing Olympics riding Orion

The Horse With Heart

Anita & Orville Unrau and Strausser

It was a snowy day when my husband, Horst, and I wound up a bumpy, narrow dirt road to a flat area where we were surrounded by Norwegian Fjord horses. Orville met us with his truck leading us up to the cutest little secluded house, with smoke winding its way up to the sky. It was so serene and idyllic. We both felt at home, nestled in our chairs with coffee and homemade soup, as we listened to the sometimes-humorous story about Unrau's wonderful driving horse, Strausser.

Anita did most of the talking while Orville scanned his laptop for dates, pictures and events pertinent to the story. He chimed in if he thought we missed something or the events needed to be explained differently.

Anita Unrau:

We started out wanting to breed the best Norwegian Fjord horse the world had ever seen. The motto of our breeding program was "Disposition, Conformation, Versatility." We started our program in the early '70s by purchasing three stallions and seventeen mares imported from their motherland of Norway. Norwegian Fjords are like small draft horses with straight legs and tough feet, bundled together with a great work ethic. They have a distinctive brown stripe that carries down their mane, back and into their tail.

Orville and I believed you could find the most beautiful horse in the world but if it did not have a sound mind and heart, you would have nothing. You would do much better to buy a horse of lesser quality as long as it had the heart and mind. A good horse needs to want to work with people and have the confirmation to stay sound.

We did everything with our horses: driving in harness, riding under saddle, pulling implements on the farm, competing in horse pulling and plowing. Many horsemen believe you cannot do horse pulling and plowing with the same horse. Our horses could do both. Our daughter would take what horse we used for driving, change its bit and take it into a riding Dressage class at shows.

Orville builds and sells competition carriages while being a trained farrier. We rounded out our income by selling our Fjords, which financed our competitions. We often travelled to the United States to meet with clients and compete.

This story begins with myself, Orville and our son Cory travelling to Cornville, Arizona. We had friends who wished to breed their mare to our stallion, while a friend of that friend wanted to purchase a couple of geldings. We always filled the trailer, so we carted along a yearling filly and a few others. While we were in Cornville, Andrea Pfeiffer called with a horse trade offer.

Andrea owned a small property with an outdoor arena, just down the road from where we were staying. She was a potter by trade. Her acreage was equipped with twelve-by-twelve stalls used to rehab injured horses. The local vets called on her to be nurse and caretaker. Doing chores and working with the horses gave her hands time to rest from pottery and was a welcome diversion. Andrea bred her two-thirds Hanoverian and one-third Quarter Horse mare to a well-known full Hanoverian stallion. The result was a three-quarters Hanoverian, one-quarter Quarter Horse red dun colt. She named him Strausser. All horses have their own unique personality and Strausser was no exception. He was aggressive and had no respect for his female owner.

Andrea did not feel emotionally tied to him and was nervous. Strausser did not like other horses either and was not friendly toward them in the pasture. Even though Andrea had a strained relationship with Strausser, she would load him up on the trailer with his head bumper on, to accompany her to deliver pottery. Strausser did not like apples much but enjoyed sharing Anita's sons' popsicles and oranges on these short trips. I am sure these snack times helped foster Strausser's acceptance of males.

Andrea took exceptional care of her colt, blanketing him and not letting his body deal with anything less than ideal footing or rain. At the first hint of rain, she would put Strausser in the barn. The year before we arrived, Strausser had thirty days of riding experience with a trainer, which was not very much. His overall training at six years-old was behind but he had frequent flyer points for trailering.

Andrea had always wanted a Fjord and desired to exchange Strausser for one of our Fjords. Orville needed to check the colt out to see if he would be a good prospect. Strausser was taken to the outdoor arena while Orville gathered his harness. The harness had many straps, including a tail crupper and blinders on the bridle. The colt stood still to be fitted then Orville gave him the command to go forward. It usually takes a horse a while to get used to the movement of the straps, surcingle and strange bridle but Strausser impressed everyone. He walked off and let Orville guide him around the arena as if he was a broke horse. Nothing seemed to bother him. Fiords were accepting of the harness but Strausser was even more so. I thought this horse wanted to be a driving horse. Our mission was complete. I left Andrea's with a box of pottery, Orville had Strausser, and we left a young Fjord filly behind.

We arrived back in Rock Creek, British Columbia, in April. It had been raining hard so the road was bogged with mud. Cory, our son, drove the truck and trailer into the driveway to find a three-foot trench. The road was washed out. We decided to take the horses out of the trailer and walk them down the road. Strausser was horrified. He had not been in rain and mud and now he found himself picking his way through both. He had already travelled without his head pumper and now he was asked to navigate his way through muck. "What is this?" he must have asked himself. Strausser's life was about to change in big ways.

Our horses lived and foraged on the rough acreage. The terrain was up and down with valleys and hillsides We supplemented their diet with hay cubes and beet pulp, but they also had to find other food on the land. Strausser had not ever foraged for himself, or been turned out on uneven terrain without sight of a building. It was a shock for him. At first he would eat the hay cubes and test out the horse balls . . . surely he had seen poop! He quickly learned they were not food and spit them out. As we left the area after chores, I would hear a clamoring of hooves with loud whinnies as Strausser ran to the top of the hill to look at the house. He needed time to acclimate and for the first year he lost weight. It was traumatic.

Orville and I determined that it was time to start Strausser's training. Orville had come upon a steep logging skid trail which he liked to drive the horses up. Strausser went up the trail, then Orville would lead him down. Strausser would go anywhere that Orville asked him to go. He always gave 110% in his training sessions. In the yard where the house was, Orville would practice tight turns. The horses were cooled down at a walk, their harness was removed and they were allowed to roll.

Strausser was being trained to do Competitive Driving and this discipline needs some explanation. The first day of competition was Dressage Day. The driving horses can be shown as an individual, a pair or team of many. They are driven pulling a carriage of either two or four wheels, into a rectangular space lined with letters. The sequence of letters is universal whether you are riding or driving. The horses are required to perform a pattern set down by the driving association. They are judged on how well the manoeuvres are executed and are awarded or scored on a penalty system. The one with the least penalty points wins. If there are enough entries, the dressage phase could span over two days. When not in the competition arena, the drivers and their navigators walk the hazard course, which is executed on the third day. The driver's job is obvious. Know your horse, carriage, the course and the rules. The navigator or "gator" rides behind the driver's seat. He or she reads the stopwatches which keep the team on the required time, and moves from side to side to stop the carriage from tipping on the tight turns. The gator shouts out their competition number to the judge at the start of each hazard. If there is a problem with the horse or carriage, the navigator can jump out to help; otherwise, he/she stays on the carriage throughout the marathon so as not to disqualify his team. The gator learns the qualities of his horse and driver. To be of the utmost assistance, he/she must know the rules of the competition and communicate effectively.

The phase with the hazards is called the marathon and is done at speed. The speeds at the lower levels are slower and get faster as you move up in the divisions. Wood fences outlining possible driving lines are called hazards. They consist of an entry point between two posts, and the letters "A" through "F" with a red and white flag on either side. The letter dictates the order the course is to be driven. The red flag must be on your right and the white on the left. The hazards include up and down hills, bridges either covered or not, water, banks, ditches, as well as sharp left and right turns.

The last day of the driving competition has to do with driving through many pairs of orange cones with a tennis ball on the top. The cones and numbers dictate where you go and in what order. The idea is to not knock over the cone or the ball on top, which would give you penalty points. The cone course is completed twice. The first time through, the competitors want to go clean, with no penalties; the second time through you need to go clean and fast.

The divisions of competition are Training A, B, C; Preliminary A, B, C; Intermediate and Advanced. Each division increases in difficulty, speed in the Marathon, and tightness of the cones. At the end of the combined days, the one with the least penalty points wins the competition. In the beginning days of competitive driving, the Marathon Day consisted of:

1) a warm-up trot, usually 15 km;

2) a ten-minute walk;

3) a fast trot of 19 km;

4) a walk; and

5) the marathon, for a total of five phases.

Several years ago, the phases other than the marathon were dropped, therefore not requiring the horses to be as fit. Horses should be trained like any other athlete.

Strausser was ready for competition. The other competitors thought he was thin, but he was starting to acclimate to his living conditions and was slowly putting on weight. We fed him grain while in training and at competition to give him extra calories.

Orville and Strausser had a lot to learn about this sport in the early years. We started Strausser in the Training division but quickly moved him up to Preliminary. They did well at Preliminary, but were making a lot of mistakes. It is all part of the learning experience.

We depended on the carriage sales to help pay for competitions and now sales were slow. With some thought, Orville decided to paint a carriage pink. I thought it was a great idea since most were painted black. We were definitely noticed when Orville showed up with his red dun gelding and his bright pink carriage.

The judge at this competition was Bill Lauer from Sea Island in Gaithersburg, Virginia. Bill took a special shine to this horse and carriage, especially when Strausser and Orville won the Preliminary division. In conversation with Orville, after all was done, he said, "You are good enough to play with the big boys. Come east. You can stay at my place." It was a surprising offer from someone Orville had just met. One we would consider.

There was always a need to make money so Orville and I accepted a job working on the movie *Eaters of the Dead* on Vancouver Island. The movie was made from the book written by Michael Crichton. The production team asked us to bring as many Fjords as we could, so we brought twenty-four plus Strausser, to make up a herd of around fifty-two horse actors. The gig lasted for three months even though the movie never went to screen. Orville worked with the horses, did stunt work and kept the horses' feet in shape. He logged in so many hours doing stunt work, he was awarded his stunt card—not that he has ever used it, but I keep his dues paid just in case. I worked on the set, as well, so we made a good amount of money. Strausser worked hard as he was ridden often by the stuntmen. Being on set may not seem like training for competition driving, but he was being desensitized to all kinds of strange items and noises.

The air and footing were moist all the time on Vancouver Island, causing the horses to get viruses and white line hoof disease (WLD). Three viruses went through the herd, so it was a busy time trying to keep all of the horses healthy during the shoot. It was September before we returned to Rock Creek.

Orville wanted to take Strausser to a significant event in Florida the following March. It was at this competition that Orville met Tom Hindenburg, who was a judge and technical delegate for driving competitions. Tom was also a competitor and for some reason needed a gator for his Morgan horse. Tom asked Orville if he would be his navigator. Tom was having issues with his horse not wanting to stand still. Orville had noticed this problem and said, "Tom you cannot let him do this. It is too dangerous." Tom asked Orville how he could fix this problem. Orville knew what to do, so he took Gus and taught him what the word "Whoa" meant. It wasn't long before Gus got the message and appeared to be "fixed."

During this challenging time with his horse, Tom had almost given up competing, so he was very thankful for Orville's training and knowledge. Again, Orville was invited to go east to Virginia and stay with Tom and Charlene. Tom said, "Stay in the house and you can put your horses in the barn."

Orville, myself and Strausser took Tom up on his offer. We stayed for three months. Tom provided a barn girl to do the chores and paid for horse feed. At first, Tom and his wife would not take any money but we eventually talked them into letting us pay for groceries. I could not believe the generosity that came our way.

I cannot remember the name of the Swiss guy who set up a cone course at Tom's. Every possible problem that you would find in competition was represented in this cone pattern. Tom and Orville practiced and practiced until the horses were going through clean. Even Gus was going flawlessly through the cones at speed. Gus had a reputation of not going clean, so this practice was making a difference. To this day, Orville gives Tom the credit for his eventual rise to the Advanced Level.

The real excitement came when the practice paid off in competition. Tom and Gus made the American team with one of Orville's carriages. The competition was to be held in Epps, Louisiana. Gus and Tom went clean on the first round of cones and were the fastest in the scurry. It was such a thrill.

Orville and I had become competitive partners with a group in Seattle. When the same people attend the same competitions, you get to know and look forward to seeing each other. It was a healthy, growing relationship. We were friends outside the competition ring, but when competing, all bets were off. We pushed each other to become better, faster and wiser. We watched each other fight to go up the levels as a competition group.

Meanwhile, we could see Strausser was getting better and better. Dressage, Marathon hazards, cones—nothing bothered him. He was starting to win even with minor mistakes in the hazards. In one competition he was the best overall competitor, prompting three top trainers to come and say, "Come work with me. I can make you faster and better. "The offers were a compliment but at this point Orville was wondering how much better could he be. He and Strausser had just beat everyone.

We were off to Atlanta where Tom Hindenburg was running the competition. Being friends, we pitched in and helped set up the numbers, flags, and the dressage ring. There was much to do and every hand was appreciated.

On competition day, we had done all right in the dressage test, so with Orville driving and I being his gator, we walked the hazard course together while Strausser relaxed in his stall munching his oats and hay. There is usually a choice in working the hazard. The rules say you have to go through the entry gate and go between the flags at each letter, but there was usually an easy slow route or a harder fast route. The water hazard had an entry point, a bridge, gentle slope, a drop into the water and the "A" gate looking right at you. At first glance it looked like one should enter, ride over the bridge, take a turn in the pool of water and go out the "A" gate. That is not what Orville saw. He saw the entry gate, a drop straight down, then out the "A" gate.

Orville looked at me and spoke softly. "I am not going over the bridge."

I said, "What?"

Orville said, "I am going to smoke this hazard. It will take way too long to come around, enter the water, go halfway around the pond and through the gate. Look at it, Anita. It is a straight line if we come in, go off that bank and exit through 'A.'"

I must have looked aghast. I said, "Do you think Strausser will do it?"

Orville replied, "Why wouldn't he?"

I reminded Orville that carriages are not meant to be airborne but Orville was determined.

My heart was in my mouth as we hit the intro gate, at the start of the water hazard. Strausser was in full gallop. Orville aimed him at the drop. Without hesitation Strausser launched off the top, hit the water and galloped out "A." It was so thrilling. I heard the crowd suddenly omit a roar, screaming and hollering. We had literally jumped our horse and wagon into the water. The rest of the gates were a blur until we had to navigate the out gate at "F." Strausser was still in a run. The carriage tipped up on two wheels, so I had to throw my weight to the left side. The outside two wheels settled to the ground; the gate was completed and Strausser settled into his fast trot. It was over and we had done it. He was so obedient that no one could touch him.

Our fellow competitors thought Orville and Strausser were the best in the Marathon but I disagreed. I believed they were best in the cones. The competitors were called, in reverse order, which meant that the last place competitor went first and so on. It was a long wait before the best horses had their time in the ring. It is nerve-racking for the drivers to see everyone else go. It would play on the driver's psyche to see another competitor have a wreck. If you saw a clean cone run, it would put pressure on you to do better. Orville didn't feel those nerves and could concentrate, usually pulling off a double clear round. Strausser always gave 110% and loved to do cones. Strausser felt Orville's confidence, which made him confident.

Orville accomplished many things in training that others did not do. He practiced a lot of sprinting forward then returning to a slower pace. Orville could listen to the cadence of the trot. Better cadence meant better ground coverage, which translated into speed. The competitors often complained at the horse park, saying the ground was too rough, the hills too steep, but for Orville and Strausser it was a piece of cake. They trained this terrain every day at home. Orville ended his sessions with tight turns in the yard of the house. He practiced homemade hazards, sprinting, slowing down, going straight. The team cooled down at the walk after each session. Strausser was unharnessed and finished his time eating grass in the yard. There was not much grass out in the field so it was a treat.

All horses have at least one thing they do not do well. For Strausser, it was his walk. He had a walk that could only be described as a zipper walk. His legs and feet were not straight. I have always said Strausser was ready to go any direction at any given point of time. Lady Sally Greyburn from Florida approached Orville and said, "Come stay with me and I will fix his walk." This world has its share of difficult people, but we had found so many knowledgeable people ready to give us a hand. It was touching and we appreciated their kindness.

Orville was interested in how Lady Sally intended to accomplish changing Strausser's walk. Lady Sally taught Orville to ask for a half halt. We put pressure on the reins just long enough for the horse to bring their mind back to the handler, then we soften the reins and allow the horse to return to their normal gait. This is done to give them a chance to rebalance, or notice that the handler is asking them to do something different. Strausser was anxious and in a hurry to get things done. The result was a quick stride, which did not cover the ground. Strausser's tension during the walk sequence made him too slow, incurring time penalties. The half halt allowed Strausser the opportunity to elongate his back and swing from the hip, resulting in a more extended ground- covering walk. This was an exercise that Orville had to do repeatedly until the half halt produced consistent results. It was a work in progress.

In this world there is often friction between those living in the west and those living in the east. Those who live in the north and those who live in the south. People become more accepting when they have a common interest, whether it be horses, dogs or children. Orville had won the Marathon in Libel, Florida. People came to congratulate him. "People I did not know," remarked Orville. Some competitors from Atlanta said they already knew that Orville and Strausser were the ones to beat before the competition started. Orville and I found that most people were positive and encouraging, no matter where they were from.

Orville was a great competitor. Being a great competitor meant he did not want to compete against teams that were not at their best. "What would be the fun in that?" Orville said. "There would be no point in beating them if they did not have their best run." Tom Chives had been doing very well in his part of the country. At the end of his preliminary year, he said, "I have won every competition but have not beaten anybody." In other words, he felt that no one challenged him. Competitors love to be challenged.

Bill Lauer had alerted Orville that a competitor's horse had lost a shoe. Just as Orville was getting ready for the Marathon, a lady named Bonnie came rushing up. She stated that it was her horse who had thrown a shoe and could Orville fix it. Orville quickly grabbed his tools and followed Bonnie. He quickly nailed the shoe back on. Bill Lauer had noticed the kind gesture and commented on how wonderful it was for competitors to help each other.

Our next stop was Indiana. After the dressage test, we were placed around the middle of the pack and now it was time to start the Marathon. Once the start signal was given, Orville, who was calm and collected, checked with me to ensure the stopwatches were synced, before he asked Strausser to pick up the trot. We would be behind the expected time for the first kilometre but by the end of the second kilometre, Strausser would have picked up the pace. By the end of the trot phase, we would be ahead of the expected time. The walk was going better than before, so we were on time. It was the third phase when things went sideways. Orville had missed his route marker and proceeded on the wrong road. Once we noticed our error we turned around and backtracked to find the marker so we could carry on, wasting precious minutes. Even with the mistake, we were early on the final walk and struck out on the marathon. This final phase was the hardest for the horses. Speeding up, slowing down negotiating the hazards. Strausser gave it his best and against all odds won that competition. This competition's outcome prompted the Combined Driving Committee to ask us to be on the Canadian driving team.

We had already been away from home since January with no thought of being asked to be on the team. It was a big decision that included our children. It was March 25th when I called home to see if the kids were willing to do the chores at home for a bit longer. The kids agreed, but informed me that I had missed my son Cory's birthday. I felt terrible and apologized. Our heads had been in the success of the sport and now we were asked to go to

Europe. Of course, the kids gave us their blessing and told us to go.

Out next stop on the circuit was Gladstone, New Jersey. For two weeks Orville stayed with the team coach. It was not a free ride for Orville. He helped out by cleaning thirty to forty box stalls every day. The coach noticed that Orville and Strausser worked hard on what he had asked them to do. Larry Brinker, a well-known Canadian horse driver, urged Orville on.

After Gladstone, it was off to Bromont, the Olympic site in Montreal. It was cold there. The horses needed to be blanketed. I am interested in natural remedies and have learned about garlic's benefits My fingers were sore from peeling so many cloves for Strausser's feed. He got a mash of beet pulp, alfalfa cubes, other herbs, kelp, celery— which is supposed to calm horses down—and, of course, lots of garlic. It is good for the immune system in people, as well as horses. He also received lots of hay, fresh water and his beloved oranges.

Training continued for Strausser. They were close to Ganaraska Park, where the drivers had a membership. They drove the trails and set up a dressage arena, along with cones to practice on.

Everything was going well. I was busy calling vets to get blood drawn for health tests so they would be allowed to fly to Europe. Then the unthinkable happened. The only thing predictable with horses is that they are unpredictable. The vet had arrived to do a routine blood draw. Most horse people can perform a blood draw themselves, but since this result was important for travel, it had to be done by an expert. It all happened so fast, I cannot tell you why, but Strausser made a misstep, slipped and landed with his back legs split apart. It was devastating. We had no idea what the extent of his injuries would be. A special FEI (Federation Equestrian International) vet had to be called, and thankfully, he was only an hour away. The FEI vet was Bernd Stanglmeier, who was a man of German descent. Bernd wanted to be a world-class vet but could not do it in the dressage and jumping world. They already had their own vets. He worked hard to be accepted into the driving world. Bernd worked his way up the ranks tirelessly. Now he is used in competitions all over.

It was difficult to tell what ligaments and other soft tissues were injured. Dr. Bernd said to hand-walk him every day and see how he was. Orville and I shared hand-walking Strausser to ensure he was under control, while moving enough to combat swelling. It was only a week before the horses were to be flown over. Strausser might make it to Europe or he might not.

A lady by the name of Elizabeth Bejerski worked with Chinese medicine. She taught me what herbs might be beneficial if added to Strausser's mash. The herbs she suggested were a mixture of stems, sticks, flowers and leaves that were ground up in a blender. At this point I was willing to try anything that might help. I think Strausser knew we were trying to help him and he ate the mixture with no hesitation.

All of the team horses were loaded on a truck and started on their way to the airport in Toronto. Among the competitors chosen to compete for Canada was John Paul Gautier, who had originally competed for France but then moved to Quebec. He was skilled and had many championships under his belt. Lucky for him, he was being sponsored by a woman in Florida, but I had to go home to Rock Creek to borrow money. We had been away for seven months without income. In the beginning, Orville had sold a few carriages and horses but the money had run out.

When transporting horses on a plane, there has to be a groom travelling with the horse boxes. Orville was that person while our daughter Sam enjoyed the trip inside the plane. Thank goodness, there were no issues during the flight. A truck met us at the airport. The horses were lifted to the ground. Strausser had his head out the window of his travel box, wind jostling his mane, ready for the next leg of his journey. We all arrived in Munich, Germany, and stabled at a farm with Orlock Trotter horses. These equines were a light-harness breed chosen for their ability to trot fast. I found them quite interesting.

Most of us thought the temperature was cold, except the girls from the Swedish team. They sat outside the barn in shorts and T-shirts while Orville had on his long johns. Except for the Swedes, the change in country and climate was hard on everyone. Our horses were all blanketed and not doing well. Canadian David Warton's Holsteiner horse was ill. John Paul had come from the heat of Florida to sixty degrees Fahrenheit in Germany, plus it was damp. JP and his horse both were not feeling well. It is for this reason that international horses arrive early, to acclimatize and have time to become strong again.

The other competitors called me a witch doctor as I continued to feed Strausser garlic. The Swedish girls thought I was brilliant and told me they always fed garlic powder and by doing so noticed their horses did not suffer from pastern dermatitis (white line disease) It is damp in Sweden just like it is on Vancouver Island. I felt Strausser had enough to deal with, healing from his accident without getting sick.

Once the quarantine period was over, we rented a truck and the horses were taken to Ebbs, Austria, not to be confused with Epps, Louisiana. They settled into their stalls at the competition site.

Strausser had a bit of a reputation for being somewhat of a junkyard dog at the competitions. He would take possession of his stall, lunging at the dividing metal bars with his mouth open. Orville put up a curtain and parked the carriage in front of his stall to protect the public. If a female groom went in to change his blanket, he would put on an ugly face and possibly threaten to bite, but if Orville went in he would say, "Come on, Strausser," and he would turn and put his head in his halter. Totally different horse.

For Orville and me, it was a dream come true. Our accommodation was a quaint little chalet. We could look out and see the mountains with low-lying fog lingering over the countryside. The land seemed different every day. We struck out on pedal bikes at 6:00 a.m. to meet our coach at the beginning of the hazard course. We were always the first ones there, giving us time to observe the church steeples looming above us, while being nestled in the valley. It was an incredible experience.

Strausser had passed the rigorous vet check but Orville knew he was not himself. This little dun horse with so much heart was doing his best under the circumstances. After the fourth hazard, Strausser did not trot straight out as usual. He placed 18th in a field of sixty or so horses after the marathon.

David was almost clear in the cones but he could not resist looking at the clock as he passed the last cone. That simple turn of his head made his horse wobble and they knocked the final cone ball off. It was disappointing.

Orville had always told me not to think when navigating, especially in the cones. I was told to sit still. When one thinks, our body starts to prepare for a turn and Strausser felt every tiny move. Strausser might mistakenly turn too soon and alter the course. Our dressage carriage sat high and I worried it would tip. That helped me to stay still. This cones course was important; every cell in my body was still, brain not thinking. The first round we were clear and now it was the scurry. The course was challenging and we were clearly watching the last two cones come closer. Orville yelled "Ha!" to encourage Strausser and then looked at the clock. He had not ever done that. Sure enough, the last ball on the last cone came down.

It was not the outcome we had wanted but none of us would have missed this experience despite the steps and money it took to get there. We felt honoured to be chosen; there was drama with Strausser's injury and now it was time to go home.

The transport arrived to take all the horses from Ebbs to the airport. Strausser was cranky and ready to go home. Orville was not travelling with the transport so he warned the driver to be careful if he needed to interact with Strausser. The driver replied, "Oh ya, ya"; his demeanour said that he was a big burly truck driver and no horse would get the better of him.

There are strict rules in Europe for hauling horses and they change regularly. A new set of regulations had just come out and the police were eager to bag themselves a rule breaker. It wasn't too long into the journey before the driver was pulled over. This police officer intently checked the travel paperwork and measured with his tape, looking to write up this trucker for some infraction of the rules. The officer then stepped up high onto the transport and opened a door into the horse's compartment. Can you guess whose door he opened? Strausser met him with a lunge and an open mouth. The officer fell back onto the pavement. He jumped up, wiped himself off, walked back to his cruiser and drove away, leaving the truck driver to have a chuckle and carry on. The driver was anxious to tell Orville of the ordeal. Orville was apologetic but the driver said," No, no, don't apologize. It turned out really well!"

The flight posed no problems. David Warton received approval from CFIA to use his place as quarantine so Strausser and the others went there. Quarantine is no picnic for very fit horses. We were required to hold the horses while their stall was being cleaned; otherwise, they had to stay put so as not to spread disease

I noticed that Strausser was selecting what he munched on for the few minutes he could. One day it was dandelions; next day leaves, next day thistles. He seemed to know what his body needed and chose that particular item or herb. He had come a long way from not knowing what apples, hay cubes or poop was.

All the Canadians were waiting for the all-clear. We had been gone since January and were anxious to go home. The horses' blood had been collected quite a while ago. The Americans had been cleared and went home a week ago.

The blood was sent to a lab in Ames, Iowa. I had lost patience and called up to ask, "What is going on?" The government was arguing with the equestrian federation over who should pay for the testing of the blood. I personally knew this lab as I had sent samples from our breeding mares there in the past.

I asked, "Well, how much does the test cost?"

The lab answered, "Twelve dollars."

I said, "I will pay the twelve dollars. Just put it on my account." In twenty minutes, the problem was resolved and the bill paid before the invoice could be printed.

The team could not believe they had been held in quarantine for weeks over a twelve-dollar lab bill. If the horses were in a commercial quarantine, the cost would be at least a hundred dollars a day. We loaded Strausser and headed home taking the northern route. Every once in a while we stopped to let Strausser get out of the trailer and stretch his legs. At one point the mosquitos were so bad, he jumped right back in the trailer, with a look of "Enough of this; let's go."

Everyone was glad to be back. Strausser went out to pasture for rest and recuperation. Orville collected one of his Fjords from Calgary, who had been in training. It was time to start a new driving horse. Strausser did not compete again.

It is hard for animal lovers to understand, but horses— unlike dogs or cats—are sold so that others can learn from an experienced horse. Strausser was thirteen years old. in 1988, Ebbs was the first World Driving Championship and Strausser had been there. He did not have to prove himself or repeat competitions with Orville.

Tom Hildenburg thought he would buy Strausser, but Strausser had other ideas. He refused to perform for Tom. Three different times we tried to sell Strausser but he sabotaged each opportunity. Strausser's big heart had found his home and he was not going anywhere.

Editor's Note:

My husband and I saw Strausser as we left the Unraus the day I completed this interview. He was happily looking over the fence in the lower pasture. As I walked up to him, he put his ears back, true to form. After all I was a woman. His eyes had seen many things and now his body was content to be at rest.

Orville and Anita's Accomplishments

- Worked on the movie set of *The Thirteenth Warrior*, starring Antonio Banderas with twenty-one of their Fjord horses

- The Unraus have been pivotal to the history of Fjords in Canada

- Orville creates and builds competition carriages for horses

A Cowboy's Jewel
Miles Kingdon and Jewel

I was born and raised on a mixed farm in southern Saskatchewan and spent my youth riding horses and looking after cattle on the family farm. I got my first horse from my parents when I was eleven or twelve years old. She was out of one of my folks' good mares, so I felt honoured to be able to work with such a fine animal. My dad helped me start this filly as a two-year-old, getting her used to the saddle, the bridle and me. Little did I know that this was the start of my lifelong career. It all came clear to me, with that mare, as I was "bit by the bug." I wanted to do more with colts and young horses, and I did. I was always trying to find a way to get them to understand what I expected of them, to know what I needed from them. Horses on the farm had a job to do, and they either made your job hard or easy depending on how well you got along with each other.

My long summer days were spent riding those prairie trails with my brother. I spent much of my time in my mind, trying to figure out a better feel with my horse—that is to say, a way of communicating with as little a signal or cue as possible. From a young age, I watched my father work with his teams. These were horses that dragged and pulled things. A team needs to feel you through the lines and understand certain words. It was expected that horses worked with word commands, which I became used to. My parents were raised in the country when a horse and buggy were used, or in the winter, a team and sleigh, which turned out to be the most reliable mode of transportation. I am proud to say so much of the way they lived has rubbed off on my brother and me.

I rode for the extensive government pastures and decided when out of high school, I wanted to ride for the big outfits year-round, so I moved out to British Columbia. During the following years, I cowboyed for Douglas Lake Ranch, Nicola Ranch, served as cow boss at Bar K Ranch, Gang Ranch, and presently, at Quilchena Cattle Co. Overall, I have been a big outfit cowboy for just over thirty years, and it has been quite a ride. I have valued my freedom dearly. I get to work in a vast, beautiful backyard full of rolling hills, valleys and flatlands. I realized some of the true treasures in my life are the memories of the people I have worked with, as well as the horses and dogs that accompanied me on my journey.

My job as cow boss is general care and maintenance of the cowherd, the horses in the outfit and the crew of people hired to work both the cows and horses. We take care of everything that pertains to the management of the grasslands, fences, water supply . . . in short, anything that makes lives better.

When I was at Gang Ranch, I had a crew of eight cowboys working with me, and each cowboy needed eight or nine broke horses in his string to keep him mounted for the year. That string of horses is called a "remuda." We had a remuda at Gang Ranch that was upwards of one hundred head of horses. Each cowboy would keep three or four of his horses in shoes for six to eight weeks at a time, then when the remuda was run in, he would change up the tired horses and shoe three or four fresh mounts.

We used near a million acres of grazing territory for the cows. Most of that being Crown-owned, grazing permit land; therefore, the crew was required to ride over a lot of ground. We would be riding thirty miles on an average day, except for four to six days off a month. The big outfits experience a significant turnover in manpower on those cowboy crews, and several of those horses may have a different rider each year. Whether younger or older, the cowboys come with varying levels of experience, not to mention personalities. Each cowboy has his own reasons for doing this job, and each rider will do the best with what he has to work with. He gets a string of horses this year, and then next year, that horse will be passed on to another cowboy. That horse will have to try to understand another mentality, another language, another way of communicating. It's not always wrong, but it's always different for the horse.

One year, I had my eye on a young mare named Jewel. She was a good-looking Quarter Horse mare who was roan in colour, which is to say that she was brown with white hairs running through her coat. Jewel had a good personality. The young fella riding her had only been on her a few times. Jewel had, at some point, acquired the bad habit of walking off when she was being mounted. This young cowboy was a pretty good rider and was trying to work with it. If he had stayed at the ranch longer and had more time, I'm sure he would have worked at changing her habit. As I said, she seemed like such a lovely young mare and a good traveller in the trailer, so when the young fella moved on, I took her in my string. She had the summer off, and I brought her in for the fall work. I liked her, and we seemed to click with each other.

It was October, and we gathered cattle from the high country. The weather was getting colder and colder each day. I woke up in my walled tent, and it was cold . . . freezing! I checked the thermometer, and it was minus thirty-three degrees. Being down in the valley, it was calm, with no wind. I had plenty of good-for-fall-weather riding wear, but I did not have time to get my winter gear from headquarters. The rest of the crew had retrieved their winter clothes and were much better prepared. I saddled up Jewel, and we rode out that morning from a calm, cold camp to the flats above, where we were met head-on with a full-blown blizzard. We had about fourteen to eighteen inches of snow on the ground at that time, and the wind was sending the snow swirling. It reminded me of a typical winter day back home. There was never a question about if there was wind on the prairies; the question was how much wind? I remember thinking, *if it's minus thirty-three degrees in camp where it is calm, I wonder what it is up here.*

Our job that day was to sort off the thinner cows and bulls, and the crew was to trail them down to headquarters to go on winter feed. The rest of the herd would trail upcountry to our fall grasslands the next day. The manager and his wife planned to meet the crew halfway on their trail with a bowl of hot stew and coffee, hoping to make their day a little better. The weather made our job a tad miserable, so it took longer to get those cows sorted off. They wanted to go brush up in the timber where the shelter was. Finally, after an hour or so, we got the sorting done, and the boys headed off with the wind to their backs. I went the opposite direction alone, since I had some cows to get from another camp before day's end.

I had ceased to really feel the bite of the cold by that time, as the fleece-lined denim jacket, leather gloves and cowboy hat did little to break the wind. I would have been fine otherwise, but before I'd gone half of a mile with the wind in my face, I knew I was in trouble. I knew that I was not adequately clothed, and I was starting to feel warm, which is a bad sign. If I got off Jewel to walk a bit, I thought I could get the blood going again and warm up, especially trudging in that snow. It's funny about hypothermia; once your body is at that low of a temperature, walking may not warm you anymore. The more I walked, the slower I got, and I realized my only hope was to get back on Jewel. Jewel wanted to get back to camp, as well, and get that harsh wind out of her face. Being a horse that liked to move, I didn't know if she would give me enough time to crawl my way back into that saddle. My body was numb and not responding well to my mind.

I found a lower spot for Jewel to stand in to gain a higher advantage. I tried to get up in that saddle but my hands could hardly hold the stirrup to get my boot started. When I reached for the saddle horn, my hand kept slipping off. I had no strength to hang on. I just couldn't seem to get my frozen fingers to grip on to anything; therefore, I didn't know how I was going to pull my body up. Repeatedly, my foot kept slipping out of the stirrup. I took a long, frustrated breath and stopped a moment to look around. My struggles had taken me to a bit of meadow inside a belt of poplar trees. The wind didn't seem to be as bad here. I thought, *So, here you are, Miles. You can't walk anymore, and you can't get in the saddle either. What a mess you have gotten yourself into.* I stopped for a moment then looked around; I was aware of what a pretty spot this little meadow was. If a fellow was to come to an end, this was not a bad place for it to happen.

Then I noticed Jewel was bumping me with her nose. She seemed to realize I was having a bit of trouble and was waiting impatiently for me to get on. She bumped me harder as if to say, "Come on, get going. It's cold out here, and you are not getting any warmer by hanging around." I made another stab at the stirrup. I put my hands around that horn and, this time, actually got my fingers locked together to get myself partway up. I did everything I could to get up there; I even hooked my chin on the horn. When I got my leg up over the cantle, which is the back of the saddle, I knew I was going to make it.

I looked sideways at Jewel's head as I shimmied my way up. She was looking at me since her nose was turned back close to my stirrup. She was seemingly willing me to get up there already and stop being such a wimp. While my left leg co-operated by staying home in the stirrup, my right leg dropped down on the right side of Jewel, and I was there. The whole time I was wrestling my way into the saddle, Jewel had not made a move. She flicked one ear back at me, then the other, and took one tiny step, then another. I spoke to her, "I'm here now, girl, and I'm staying here." With that, she moved off at a walk and then a little jog once she knew I was stable. I couldn't hold the reins, so I just trusted that she would find her way back to camp. The pace seemed to be good for my body. It was not long before I could see the camp. The lights were on, and a trail of smoke from the fire spiralled up to the night sky. We travelled down the hill, out of the horse pasture, into the slight hollow of the camp. We were out of the wind, and it felt so much warmer.

Jewel stopped at the haystack, and I slid out of the saddle. I looked at her, and she looked at me. "I wouldn't have made it without you, girl," I told her. She blew out her nose and grabbed a mouthful of hay. I managed to hobble my way to the cookhouse. I cupped some hot coffee while other cowhands took care of Jewel. We were both happier.

Horses, dogs, cowboys—they came into my life, and they moved on. I can't help thinking of the horses I have ridden. When I have gotten myself into a predicament, and it happens in this lifestyle, I am always thankful that my horse was there with me. It is good if your horse likes to be around you, and if they don't, you may have a long walk home.

I have ridden several horses in different outfits. Sometimes I stop when I'm tapped out on a ridge somewhere looking at the mountains, sitting on another promising horse, and wonder whatever became of this one or that one.

I think fondly about Jewel and the time I almost froze myself on that ride. She helped me out when I needed her most. The following summer, some other cowboy will benefit from riding her. At the Gang Ranch, Jewel will live out her days with the freedom of all that country to roam in. She is definitely a Jewel of a horse.

*"Your own imaginations become visions, and
your own visions become your own dreams and
your own dreams become your own reality."*
—Miles Kingdon

Miles Kingdon's Accomplishments

- Respected trail boss and knowledgeable horseman

- Inducted into the BC Cowboy Hall of Fame, 2017

- Author of *"A Cowboy's Story"*

- Miles continues to teach clinics, workshops and customized training on horsemanship

The Gentle Giant

Larry Brinker and Goldherr

Larry Brinker started his career in the equestrian world at twelve years old. I was surprised to learn he started competing in Western Games, then Rodeo/Calf Roping. Almost like a politician crossing the floor to the opposition, he decided to go English—competing in Show Jumping, Eventing, Combined Driving and FEI Dressage.

Larry often was my dressage judge at the events. He was fair and known for not giving high marks unless you deserved them. I am sure he has no memories of myself and Ambiance. The last dressage test I rode for Larry was in Campbell Valley outside of Langley, where my horse prematurely stepped out of the ring, causing an immediate disqualification.

I knew that Larry had a diverse background in all things equine, including driving horses in competition. It was through Larry that I learned about Orville and Anita Unrau. He gladly gave me his story of Goldherr.

Larry Brinker:

Goldherr, a black Bavarian Warmblood, was born in Germany and, like many young warmbloods, was offered for sale at a three-year-old auction. A Canadian family purchased him, along with two other horses. As luck would have it, he was purchased before the auction, but according to the rules his number could not be omitted; he was put through the sales ring, and the Canadians were told to continue bidding until he was sold. The young horses were put through a jumping shoot as part of the display. The big, almost eighteen-hands three-year-old went down the jumping chute over the balance poles, took four strides and went over the four-foot-six-inch oxer. The auction staff quickly raised the oxer to five feet six inches with a six-foot spread. Goldherr cantered into the jumping lane, jumped over the balance poles, took four significant strides and cleared the oxer with room to spare. Then, with several ground-covering powerful strides, he also cleared the six-foot retaining wall and left the sales ring, landing in the adjoining parking lot! He was brought back into the ring and the bidding was electric! Goldherr received the highest price of the auction.

Imported into Canada, Goldherr found his new home in northern British Columbia, where his excited owners set about training him to be a jumper. Here, a tiny problem arose due to his rapid growth; he was neither strong nor terribly well-coordinated. He found that jumps tended to move out of his way if he hit them hard enough with his chest. Exasperated, his owners sold him. Goldherr gained an undeserved reputation as a problem horse. Subsequently, he was sold several more times until he all but refused to step over a pole on the ground or to even go forward.

One day a lady looking for a large, gentle horse came upon him, took pity on his obvious plight and offered to purchase him. The owner asked what she was willing to pay and was told $4000.00 (which topped out the old VISA card). The offer was accepted, and his saddle and bridle were thrown in for good measure. Goldherr's luck was about to change.

Goldherr was lightly ridden by the lady and several of her friends. A young man began to work with Goldherr, and with patience and kindness, the horse started to come around. The pair moved to Vancouver, BC, and started to compete in Dressage. Here, the rider felt he needed a more experienced horse, so he looked into returning Goldherr to his home up in northern BC. The shipping cost was steep, so on an off chance, he phoned me to see if I needed a big horse to ride. Since I am six foot four inches, and an eighteen-hand horse is not too big, I tried the then eight-year-old gelding.

Goldherr was not the most attractive nor the most balanced horse I had ever ridden, but there was something in his attitude toward me that seemed to say, "Take me—I'll try my best for you." So, I phoned the owner, organized a lease to train the horse and took him to my home in late November. It promptly snowed—a rarity—and even rarer, the snow stayed for six weeks . . . too cold and slippery to ride. I finally started a regular riding program with the horse in late March.

The first show of the season was the first weekend in May. Goldherr and I entered our first dressage test equivalent to Level One, Test Four and came out with a score of 73.3%. Suddenly we were the pair to beat! Our success continued that year, and we placed Canadian Reserve Champion at our level.

The following year, we moved up to the equivalent of Third Level in the USDF (United States Dressage Federation) tests. We really were the team to beat that year, winning championships at five shows.

The Canadian Championships were held at the stable where Goldherr had started his early Canadian jumper training. We moved in the day before the competition, as usual. I took another of my horses out for some exercise and left Goldherr by himself in his stall. Shortly after, a friend came running to the ring and stated, "Get back to the barn fast!" I went right away to find Goldherr in a sweat, throwing himself against the stall walls hard enough to crack a six-by-six-inch beam. My wife met me at Goldherr's stall where he rushed over and put his head around my shoulders. His whole body was shaking. I took him out of his stall and walked around the grounds for a couple of hours. He settled; I fed him and put braids in his mane for the next show day, groomed and talked to him. At about 10 p.m., I decided to go back home for the night and rest. Goldherr would not let me leave his stall; he stood in front of the door. If I tried to leave, he would grab my coat sleeve with his teeth. Finally, at about 11 p.m., I told him that I promised to be back early and that no one would touch him in the interim. I decided to move my wife's little pinto into the next stall for his security and disassemble the adjoining wall to chest height. It worked, and he let me leave.

The next day I returned to his stall, tacked him up and led him to the warm-up ring. Goldherr seemed to be all right and warmed up nicely. The competition ring was the same ring in which he had been taught to jump. As horse owners, we often wonder if horses recall when they have had questionable treatment. As soon as we trotted into the arena, Goldherr became rigid. No matter what I did, the tension never left his body for the remainder of the test; we finished a disappointing fourteenth. At the bottom of a dressage test the judge can leave comments concerning the ride. The comment correctly pointed out how tense the ride was. Not a comment we had received before.

I tried not to be downhearted as we worked over the winter and started the next season at Fourth Level. We won the championship cooler in every show we entered, again, becoming the team to beat. Competing at the Canadian Championships, we were Canadian Reserve

Champion in our test and Canadian Champion in the Fourth Level Musical Freestyle!

We bumped up to Prix St. George Level in the following year with a fair amount of success, some wins and many seconds. When the "fancy" horses were on their game, they could beat us, but one slip and we had them. Goldherr was steady and consistent.

The following year Goldherr and I went Advanced for the first time. We won the Prix St. George and were second in the Intermediare, but total points gave us our first Advanced Championship cooler! We also made the long haul to the major West Coast Dressage Competition in Parker, Colorado. Goldherr was a star with his extraordinary presence and gentleness. He proved to be a favourite with both competitors and spectators, to the point the Denver media dubbed him "The Gentle Giant."

That year, based on our results, Goldherr and I were long-listed to the Canadian dressage team, a feat we would repeat the next year as well.

In the last competition I rode with Goldherr, we competed in our first-ever Grand Prix. We scored 56%. Not a big score, but I was excited to be at this high level. Goldherr had given me this chance of a lifetime.

The following spring, my wife and I said our bittersweet goodbyes to Goldherr, sending him to a new owner in Dayton, Ohio. We had made sure that he would be loved and pampered, to the same degree or more than we had done. It's okay, though; he has earned every pet and treatment given to him. Goldherr, as I write this, lived to a ripe old age. He retired to a sunny pasture outside Ocala, Florida, with the lady who bought him from me. He indeed was a great horse.

Larry Brinker's Accomplishments

- English certified coach and trainer up to the FEI level in Dressage and Driving

- Three-Day Event coach and official.

- Course designer for hunters and jumpers

- Officiates Combined Driving competitions

- Served in numerous capacities with national and local equestrian organizations, filling almost every position in horse competition management

The Little Horse That Could
Nick Holmes-Smith and Country Yucca

My first contact with Nick came when I competed with an Appaloosa horse named Ezekiel. I remember driving into Chase Creek and being stunned by the sheer beauty of the countryside. The trailers, cars and trucks were parked in a flat field bordering a wooded area that sheltered the rustic stabling for the horses. Chase Creek (the stream, not the site) meanders its way behind the stalls, giving the place a serene, if not mystical, feeling. No matter where you gaze, treed hills cradle the site in a valley. To this day, I will never forget the times I was blessed to be at this venue.

Ezekiel was often stabled right next to the actual creek. I affectionately called this location the "Hilton." I was jealous that the babbling water lulled him while I bedded down in a field.

My memories of Nick consisted of the times I attended his clinics. He is not tall, but he walked and talked with purpose and authority. At the beginning of our class, riders and horses gathered around him with anticipation and excitement about what the day would hold. Nick would address each of us to find out our background and the history of our horses. He would tell us what he expected and give us a synopsis of what we would accomplish for the day. At some undetermined point, he would utter, "Enough talk, let's go do it." If you were expecting tedious technical jargon, then you were at the wrong clinic.

Nick's talent and experience came in as he quickly assessed what your horse could do, and he would send you to jumps that were within your level but might test your level of fear. There was no patience for those who refused to take instruction. Nick's philosophy was that you paid to jump cross-country jumps, and that is what you were going to do—leave your dressage saddle at home and bring your best game face. I trusted him implicitly with my well-being. I believed him and galloped down to the obstacle if Nick said I could do it. My horse Eekie was equally excited to be on course, and rarely did he refuse to jump. Both of us gained courage and experience at Chase Creek, which helped us win the first-ever Training Clinic. Nick and others designed the Training Clinic to give riders experience on a full-fledged three-day event which consisted of two roads and tracks, steeplechase and a veterinarian check box. The higher Preliminary Level was the usual first taste of a complete phase event. The committee decided to introduce all phases at the Training

Level. Rules being rules, Nick had to call the event a clinic to make it "legal" and allowable by Equine Canada.

I enjoyed Nick's "go get 'em" attitude with little attention to detail. He conducted business in the same way and had definite opinions on how things should be. His daughters are now taking up the torch and competing in the Three-Day Event discipline.

This story is about Nick's first great horse, Country Yucca, a pony in stature. Ally, Nick's wife, has carried on with an amazing pony named Paddington Bear, with whom she competed up to the Intermediate Level. Nick and his family have been an inspiration in the discipline of Horse Trials and Three-Day Eventing in British Columbia, but enough talk, let's move on to Country Yucca.

Nick really did not like horseback riding in the beginning. Like most horse-crazy people, his sister Susan, walked, talked and breathed horses. Skiing was Nick's first passion. When he was riding, his mother insisted that he don tight stretchy pants and wear a funny-looking black hard hat, and then there was that sissy little English saddle. In the '70s, it wasn't cool to ride horses in an English saddle; in rural British Columbia, 80% of riders rode in a Western saddle and chased cows. Girls rode English, and that was fine with Nick. Being a boy, he had to endure the teasing from some of the guys at school and longingly watched the other boys playing baseball from the opposite side of the fence. He wondered how he ended up in this embarrassing sport and secretly wanted out. The galloping and jumping were fun, but all the work with owning a horse seemed tedious. The flatwork was just plain dull. Nick's mother, Rosemary, was a committed horse person and had the ways and means to guide her children in this direction. Nick didn't want to disappoint his mother, so he continued riding.

In the beginning, Nick had a string of rather obnoxious and untalented horses and ponies. The first was a medium-sized, un-athletic grey Anglo/Arab mare. In his first horse trials, Nick had twenty-two refusals and two falls. The ground crew kept whistling him out, but he just kept kicking this dishonest pig of a pony around the course, using excessive amounts of foul language while flailing his short, ineffective riding crop. Interestingly, Nick was not discouraged but became keener to event, even though there were not many clear rounds or great victories in the beginning. The bright star in the early years was a terrific Welsh/Arab mare by the stable name of T-bag. Her show name was Turis Hill Tina, and she gave him a taste of success. This dynamite little pony was passed on to others after Nick to teach many aspiring athletes to ride and enjoy the sport.

Yucca was born at Country Farms, owned by the Irwin family in Fraser Valley, British Columbia. In the Western Show Horse discipline, as you show your horse and receive ribbons, you also get points, which add value to your breeding stock. Yucca King was a stallion who earned several grand championships to his credit: Halter, Cutting, Trail Horse, Western Pleasure and Reining. A document stated that Yucca King sold for $50,000.00, a hefty sum of money. The Irwins bred their champion American Quarter Horse stallion to a mixed breed mare who was a quarter Thoroughbred, a quarter Quarter Horse, a quarter Saddlebred and a quarter Standardbred. She was a true Quarter Horse if there ever was one. This foal was the first Bill and Sharlis Irwin had raised. They called her "Baby." She grew into quite a talented horse in her own right, being ridden several times on the Fraser Valley Hunt with Bill. Baby carried—or in technical jargon, packed out—many deer killed in the hunt. Baby lived to the ripe old age of thirty-three. They buried her on the hillside overlooking the mountains, on the Irwin property. Baby and Yucca King were the proud parents of Country Yucca. The day Yucca introduced himself to the world, he looked exactly like his award-winning father, who was black with a large paint splash of white on his face and four white stockings. Both parents had great athleticism, and the genes lined up perfectly for this little dynamo of a colt.

There was not much written about Yucca in his early years, but his life was about to become very exciting, and he was ready for whatever came his way. His first owner was an up-and-coming dressage rider by the name of Leslie Reid. Leslie's mom, Edie, was looking for a suitable mount for her child to jump and learn more about the equestrian game. This cute, loveable pony seemed perfect even though he was exuberant. Leslie rode jumpers at the time, so Yucca was introduced to what would later become his remarkable talent. Leslie grew too tall for Yucca, and she sold him to her friend Jackie Gill. Jackie did everything Pony Club offered with Yucca and then passed him to Judy Thompson, whose passion was show jumping but who competed in Three-Day Eventing.

At this point, you might be wondering how this large pony was handling the different owners, the different riding styles and the different disciplines. Yucca was a no-nonsense kind of equine. "Just point me at it and let me go" was his mantra. Nothing was too big, wide or scary for him. Yucca measured just one-sixteenth of an inch above the allowable 14.2 hands. The rules state that under 14.2 hands is a pony, and over 14.2 hands is a horse. If Yucca could look in a mirror, he would not see himself as a pony but would have seen himself as an eighteen-hand majestic horse. That was his mentality. His ears were constantly forward, and his mind was full tilt ahead. *Bring it on, and I will carry my rider with pride and courage!*

Judy was competing at the Preliminary Level in Calgary when Nick Holmes-Smith's mother, Rosemary, saw him, and he won her heart. She quickly made a deal to purchase Yucca with her son in mind. For Nick, Yucca was a game changer.

Rosemary knew her son would need a tough-minded, talented mount. So it was that Nick, who was a "ride 'em cowboy, get the job done" kind of a teenager, found Yucca, who was a "leave me alone and let me do my job" type of horse. When he got off the little grey mediocre ponies and got onto the black-and-white Quarter Horse, he had thought that he had died and gone to heaven. Nick couldn't believe that a horse and the sport of riding could be so wonderful. As it turned out, it would be a while before Nick and Yucca would work their magic together in the show ring.

Yucca's first show was with Susan, Nick's sister, on Vancouver Island. It seems that being Nick Holmes-Smith had its trials and tribulations. Diving into a swimming pool, Nick aimed for the hole in a rubber inner tube and ended up hitting the side of the pool with his head. Recovery was in order, so Susan rode Yucca in the BC Championships and finished third.

The Holmes-Smiths were pleased with their new purchase and waited patiently to see their son in action. It was 1976 and time for the Western Canadian Games, so the young Nick and his pony headed for their first big competition. Neither Nick nor Yucca enjoyed the Dressage phase. Except for being a little shy at the flowers, the two finished well and looked forward to Cross-Country. Well, it didn't rain, but it hailed, making the ground wet and soggy. Being the first ones on the course was advantageous since the footing was still intact. When the conditions are poor, the riders depend on their horses to be agile and safe. Yucca rose to the challenge and kept himself and his rider from harm. As they came off the course with a clear round, someone shouted, "What's the course like?' Nick answered, "Piece of cake." He owed it all to his new partner. Team BC won the gold.

On the last night of the competition, Yucca was stabled next to lions, tigers and elephants. It seems like the circus had come to town. It was a rough night for the pony, surrounded by strange smells and even stranger bedfellows. The next day brought a whole new set of experiences.

The Alberta team headed to Toronto for the Continental Young Riders competition. They needed one more rider and asked Nick and Yucca to complete the foursome. It was off to the airport so Yucca could catch a plane ride. The original plan was for horse transport to take the team, but there was an outbreak of encephalomyelitis in Manitoba. The province did not allow the horses to drive through. Their coach, Robert Coates, twisted the Alberta government's arm sufficiently to make them fly the horses to Ontario!

Money had come through to fly the horses, but the riders had to find their way. Setting out on his own and probably not too knowledgeable on how big Canada was, Nick ended up hitchhiking from British Columbia to Ontario for the big show. Nick remembers a particularly wet night where he huddled under a bridge. There were a few car rides, but this night found him lonely and soggy. As he huddled to keep warm and feeling miserable, he heard the sound of a jet. He thought of his beloved pony in a warm, dry place, smiling as he made his way overhead. Something was wrong with this picture.

Nick and Yucca were united in Toronto, and the cross-country course was challenging. The riders get to walk their route ahead of time while the horses calmly munch hay back in their stalls. During the walk, strategies and approaches to jumps are discussed. There were few technical areas that included multiple jump efforts in the early years of Eventing. Nick remembered a ditch at this particular competition followed by a half coop. This combination required the horse to jump the broad ditch, land and immediately jump the coop with no canter stride in the middle. In training, we called this a bounce jump. Nick admitted that he didn't really have to do much while negotiating the jumps. "I just pointed Yucca in the direction of the obstacles and let him choose the pace, which was always fast," he says. It was so fast that Nick didn't feel the brief encounter Yucca should have made with the ground when they came to the ditch and the coop. Nick realized as they galloped away that Yucca cleared the two jumps in one mighty leap. This stunt would have been outstanding for the largest horse at the competition; it was inconceivable for a pony. This would not be the last time Yucca would do the impossible.

There has been much talk about the old Kelowna cross-country course in the eventing world. This venue was used when there were not so many rules and regulations, so the jumps were big and scary. There was a jump that was affectionately called the suicide drop. Many horses refused. This jump separated the meek from the brave or otherwise insane.

With the suicide drop safely behind them, Yucca and Nick galloped down to the sunken road. The idea was to come to the edge and jump down onto the road; the horse took one canter stride and jumped up the other side. Nick was confident and rode forward, although he could feel Yucca sizing up the situation. Usually, horses slow down when they are unsure of a jump, especially when there are technical elements. Nick lifted his shoulders, planting his seat deeper into the saddle, waiting for the change of pace, but it didn't happen. Instead, Yucca ramped up and charged full speed ahead. There was no drop, no stride and no jump up. Yucca took one mighty leap and cleared the whole thing to the gasp of the small crowd. The little pony who could cleared close to twenty-six feet. Look at all the time he saved by not doing that dilly-dallying around with extra efforts.

By this time, Nick and Yucca were the talk of the town. Talented horses were said to have scope, meaning that they had the athletic ability to jump high and wide. Yucca was unlike any horse that Nick had ever seen. The term "scopey" was an understatement for this little wonder horse. He could and would jump anything from any distance. This gave Nick all kinds of confidence. Like all good riders, he was still taking lessons and getting coaching. It was suggested that Nick take more control of his mount and start dictating the speed and the take-off spot in front of the jump. Like all good students, he endeavoured to do what he was told. During this change, Nick noticed that Yucca wasn't jumping like he used to. The courses were not riding well, and the two were making mistakes. Finally, Nick figured it out. It was not Yucca's way to be told what to do. He knew his job, and he loved to jump, but it had to be his way or the highway. After a trial time of doing, it "right," Nick dared to let Yucca have his head and make decisions. This method worked for them.

Three-Day Eventing is exhilarating in good weather, but it is downright anxiety-building when the weather is less than cooperative. This was the older days of eventing when the rules for jump sizes and water depths were much different from today. The technical delegate arrives early to measure the jumps to ensure they are within the rule book's specifications and to make sure the footing is safe. There have been many changes to make the courses safer for the riders and especially for the horses. No matter how much the organizers do to prevent problems, Mother Nature has a way of storming in and changing the equation.

It was Susan's turn to ride Yucca at the Fraser Valley Event. It had rained heavily all night, making the footing slippery. The water jump was a stream that trickled through the middle of the course. The riders had walked through it the day before, checking the depth and the safety of the creek bed. Susan and Yucca were challenging the wet course, and since Yucca had no issues with water, Susan was confident the stream crossing would be no problem. When you're galloping down to an obstacle, there is little time to make rash decisions. As they approached the water, Susan could see that it was much higher than the day before. The downpour had turned the stream into a raging river. How high could not be gauged. She urged Yucca on, and he plunged in. Most water jumps you can gallop through, but in this case, there was no bottom to be had. Yucca would have to swim. Susan held on with all her might, trusting that Yucca would go in the right direction and get them to dry land. He climbed out and galloped on as if this was a regular everyday occurrence.

There was no end to the surprise of what Yucca could do. Nick arrived at the prestigious Radnor Hunt Horse Trials in Pennsylvania. There is much to do when a competitive pair arrive at the show grounds. Stalls need to be bedded; tack must be sorted and hung up. There's the mandatory trip to the show office to get your number and find out what time you ride. During the hustle and bustle, one cannot help but look at the arriving horses and compare his/her mount to the others. Unbeknownst to Nick, the ground jury—part of the event officials—looked at Yucca getting out of the trailer. They were not aware of his talent and the successes that he already had in Canada. The pair were entered in the Intermediate Division. The course designers had made the route difficult. They were concerned that this pony would be over-faced and possibly injured. The dressage test was the most challenging for Yucca, so he was glad to get that done. He flew over the Cross-Country clean and dry, putting himself in a respectable twelfth position.

Over the years, the two crossed Canada six times for different competitions, so long trips were not unusual. They found themselves in Alberta, returning from Oklahoma, where the Continental Young Riders competition took place. It was 1976, and the team was overnighting in the sleepy, windswept town of Brooks, Alberta. The horses were corralled at the Brooks Veterinary Clinic, just off the Trans-Canada Highway. Everyone was tired and ready to settle down for the night after the horses were fed, watered and tucked in. They left the horses blanketed and bandaged to be prepared for the next day of travel.

Funds were tight, so the riders stayed in their vehicles and campers. As the cobwebs of sleep were settling in, there was an unmistakable sound of hooves on the pavement— not just one set but several. Nick jumped out of his Suburban, pulling on his jeans and seeing the unthinkable. The entire BC team of horses was trotting single file down the main drag of Brooks, led by the proud and fearless leader of the pack, Country Yucca. Every emotion came to the surface as the horse owners grabbed halters and ran for the street. They tried to flag down the few vehicles that were passing by, but most veered around the disheveled-looking group that were waving their arms and ropes, clad in pajamas.

Finally, some brave soul stopped, and everyone piled into his vehicle and screamed, "Follow those horses!" The sight of the horses heading down the Trans-Canada was almost too much to endure. Yucca led his herd into the parking lot of an all-night truck stop. They must have looked like a bunch of equine hitchhikers with their blankets and leg bandages, all ready to go.

Slowly and cautiously, the horses were approached with a joint chorus of "Whoa, steady now." As every horse person knows, settling horses that are heightened with excitement is not an easy thing. Surrounding the herd might have worked if it was not for the devilish ringleader. Yucca whirled, kicked the air with his hind hooves and was off again. There was a lot of scurrying and swearing as everyone jumped back into the chase vehicle. The one good thing is that they were heading back toward the medical clinic.

The few people who had stayed behind saw the horses heading their way. They thought they had made an effective barrier to guide the horses back to the yard using their bodies. Yucca's white face was shining in the moonlight as he continued his purposeful trot, right past the well-meaning troop.

Next to the clinic were the sacred grounds of the Brooks cemetery. You guessed it; Yucca led his merry band into a place where there was plenty of grass for all.

The horses disappeared into the darkness in amongst the tombstones. The horrified riders headed into the pristine and hallowed grounds to be greeted by the silhouettes of horses against the night sky, grazing happily amongst the deceased.

There was no thought of fixing the multitude of divots made by the iron-clad hooves. They caught their steeds, walked them back to the veterinary clinic, sheepishly loaded them up and left town. Nick admitted later that Yucca was known for using his nimble lips to lift his door latch and get out of his stall. This would not be the first or the last time Yucca would escape and cause some excitement.

The two were competing at the Intermediate Level, which was an amazing feat for such a petite horse. The next division up was Advanced. At the Advanced Level, horses are chosen for the Olympics

it was 1978 when Yucca travelled to Calgary, where the candidates for the Canadian team would be considered. Yucca was familiar with this course. Being a small horse, he could tuck himself into a tight ball and bounce over the fences, knowing just where to land. It was unbelievable, but he won.

Nick and Yucca made their way to Jokers Hill, Toronto. It was Yucca's first Advanced course, and he handled it like a pro. At this level of competition, some horses were obviously at the top of their game. It was sheer guts and determination that got them around fault-free on cross-country day. Nick remembers Yucca flying over the gruelling course with unprecedented athleticism. Even if Nick came into a jump and Yucca decided to take off far away from the base of the jump, it was as if he sprouted wings and had jet-propelled legs. The pair finished seventh and qualified for the Canadian Equestrian Team (CET).

The coach of the Canadian team decided that Yucca had to prove himself one more time. In Chesterland, USA, there was a shortened version of an Advanced course. Yucca was tired, but if he was going to have a definite spot on the Olympic team, he would have to run Advanced one more time. Yucca jumped his heart out, but something happened on the very last fence. Disaster had struck. He finished the course but, in a few hours, he came up lame. Yucca had bowed his front tendon. A bow is when the large tendon ruptures out of the sheath that holds it together. The injury was severe, and Nick knew right there and then that his Olympic dream with his little horse could not be realized. If only there had been more time to rest between the competitions.

Rosemary was devastated that her son's dreams were dashed, but her concern was directed toward Yucca. She wanted to help him heal as best he could from his injury. Yucca was shipped to Ontario's prestigious Guelph Veterinary College. He was poked and prodded by aspiring young vets. One day he was jumping the best combinations in the world, and now he was stuck in a ten-by-ten box stall with bandages and topical ointment. Yucca amused himself by escaping his wood–and–metal prison. He had a good look around the university grounds before his frustrated keepers were able to catch him.

Yucca returned to Oliver with Rosemary. She had bandaging and progressive exercise to do every day if Yucca was to return to the job he loved most.

By spring, the bowed tendon had stabilized, and Yucca started slowly back into work. He would never again be the Olympic hopeful. Still, he could compete at the Training Level with young riders. What a blessing to use this experienced horse. Yucca travelled with Nick. Possibly it was hard for Yucca to see Nick go off and ride another horse.

It was decided that the Annual General Meeting for Horse Trials, would be held in one of Oliver's hotels. The awards were given out to those who had received the highest points for the summer's competitions. Two horses were to be honoured and recognized for their high level of achievement.

As the names were read out, the two double doors that led into the banquet hall were opened, and Country Yucca was ushered in by his beloved Nick. Country Yucca was sidelined by injury, but his heart had reached many in the equestrian community. He stood there while everyone clapped and stood up in honour of this horse with a big heart and even bigger talent. A lady dashed up to Yucca, flung her arms around his neck and kissed him while pictures were taken. The president of the Bank of British Columbia's wife was selected to give out the evening's awards.

Yucca retired, sort of, after that night. Some others could take advantage of his training as he did go to other competitions at the lower levels. Nick eventually lost track of where Yucca ended up or when he actually died.

Editor's Note:

As I prepared to write this story, I talked to many of those still active in the eventing world, and the name Country Yucca is still remembered and talked about. Nick remembers him as his first real taste of success. He remembers the connection they had in spirit and mind. Yucca showed Nick what competing at a high level felt like, and he drew out the talent in Nick for him to go on and compete at two Olympics for Canada. Nick's sister called Yucca "Houdini in Horse Clothes" for his many escape episodes. Those escapes attested to his intelligence and game sense.

Nick divides the horses he has owned and ridden over the years into different attitudes they possess. First, there are the horses that totally dislike jumping. Most often, these horses merely do not have the conformation that allows them to quickly negotiate fences. They find jumping awkward and uncomfortable, so they don't like to do it. Sometimes horses are physically able to jump but just don't enjoy it; usually, these are the same horses that don't like doing anything at all. Next are the horses that jump willingly, but primarily out of obedience, not passion. They jump when asked, get the job done, and that is all there is. The final category is the horses that absolutely LOVE to jump. Country Yucca was at the extreme end of this category. He lived and breathed to jump fences. A lot of humans are like that too, Nick says. They love getting "air." It could be on a bike, skis or a trampoline. Getting air is fun . . . and Country Yucca loved to get big air. Nick went on to bring to our attention while talking about big air that Yucca was fourteen hands two inches, and young Nick was small for his age when he first started riding Yucca. At sixteen years old, Nick had grown to five feet, nine inches and 165 pounds, which made him rather large for a pony. Yucca was small but chunky, being a Quarter Horse. He weighed in at about 1000 pounds. Yucca carried Nick with no problem, which attested to his strength, scope and jumping ability.

Wherever you rest, Yucca, know that your story goes on, and you have made your mark in the equestrian community, and you have taught one of its finer riders and coaches.

Nick Holmes-Smith's Accomplishments

1988 –   Seoul Olympics

1992 –   Gold at Pan American Championships in Chatsworth, Georgia

1992 –   Barcelona Olympics (Team and Individual Events)

Nick and his wife, Ali, own and operate a Three-Day competition site in– between Chase and Falkland, British Columbia.

My Partner Quincy

Jonathan Field and Quincy

Jonathan is a well-known coach of natural horsemanship in British Columbia. He trains horses and helps people to become one with their horses. In this story, not only does he not give up on a difficult horse, but he understands that this horse could teach him—a lesson we all need to learn as trainers and coaches.

Johnathan Field:

Quincy is a super horse to the extreme: athletic, powerful, fast. He has incredible endurance and strength, in addition to being reactive, spooky and ultra-sensitive. He can bolt and reach up to the sky with his rearing ability, too. These "super" attributes certainly have their pluses and minuses.

I'll never forget the first time I saw Quincy, on the first day of a weekend clinic at Spencer Stables in Abbotsford, BC. As I was setting up to facilitate a clinic, Quincy came through the arena door and stopped in my tracks. He was a stunning silver horse with a regal presence. Clearly an athlete, his body was muscular and well conformed. His head was held high, acutely aware of his surroundings. Quincy's eyes darted back and forth, taking in everything around him. There was something special about that horse which I couldn't express in words, but the feeling was almost overwhelming.

A week earlier, I had received a call from Karen, an experienced rider who had discovered that her recently purchased gelding was more than she had bargained for. The smallest of stimuli would send this horse into a complete frenzy. He would rear without hesitation, bolt and run away before Karen could even blink. Determined to give him a fair chance, she contacted me and together, we arranged for her to attend my next clinic.

The class started, and as I was teaching the eleven students, my radar kept focusing on Quincy. It was important that I understood Quincy's behaviour, and I formulated a plan to make a difference to this challenging animal. I wanted to help Quincy find the key for Karen to succeed with him.

After lunch, I asked the students to send their horses out on a circle, then rub them with the horseman's stick. Out of the corner of my eye, I saw Quincy rear up on his powerful hind legs and shoot backwards twenty feet in the blink of an eye. He nearly yanked off Karen's arm in the process and almost bulldozed two other students and their horses. This guy could really rear—so much so that it looked as though he would flip over. A hazardous situation for the horse and Karen.

I took Quincy from Karen as the other students darted quickly out of harm's way. She explained that she had tried to rub Quincy with the stick, just as she had been doing all morning, but this time he chose to explode into the air.

I sent Quincy out on a circle; after he had trotted for a few moments, I reached in to give him a rub with the horseman's stick. He reared instantly and bolted backward as if I had just tried to pet him with a live rattlesnake.

At this point, I could have moved on to different things and ignored the rub with the stick because he didn't like it. However, avoiding this reaction would only reinforce Quincy's belief that reacting was a way to avoid doing something he didn't want to do. Instead, my plan was to continue approaching and retreat with the stick until I could touch him with it.

I explained the process of desensitization to my students, emphasizing the "release" once the horse began to relax. When Quincy had a massive reaction to the stick, I would back off a little, but I wouldn't altogether remove it. I observed his response and waited for Quincy to begin to relax. At the slightest sign of acceptance, I would stop and give him a rest. It went on for over an hour. He had worked himself into a sweat, but I was able to get him to stand while I rubbed his shoulder with only a slight reaction from him.

This pattern of huge reactions to the simplest things was a bleak road for Quincy. It was only a matter of time before he seriously hurt someone during one of his blind explosions. I knew that Karen wouldn't be the one to end his life, but undoubtedly down the road—as he would go from home to home—he was bound to end up at the auction or the slaughterhouse. I was aware that the only reasons he had made it this far were his good looks and potential. Karen admitted this clinic was her last hope for Quincy because he was simply too much for her at this point in her life.

For the rest of the weekend, I continued to keep everyone safe and carefully worked around Quincy's issues. His unpredictability was a danger to Karen and the surrounding students. The riders had an unspoken agreement to stay at least twenty feet away from Karen and Quincy. When the group started the riding exercises, Karen continued to practice the skills from the ground because Quincy would not stop rearing. She was definitely safer on the ground than in the saddle.

By the end of the weekend, Quincy had not progressed nearly as far as I had hoped; I needed to focus equally on all the students in the group, which certainly didn't leave enough time to address all of the issues with Quincy. I really wanted to help both Karen and the horse. So, I offered to do some private training at my farm after the clinic.

When we met the following morning, Karen mentioned that one of Quincy's biggest fears was plastic bags. This would be a good training tool to test him, giving me an idea of his responsiveness. As I do with every horse, I would take all the time Quincy needed to make a positive change. In the back of my mind, however, I was thinking that it wouldn't take more than an hour or two. It's been my experience over the years that even the most difficult horses didn't need more than an hour to become desensitized to a plastic shopping bag.

A critical aspect of using an approach and retreat method for desensitizing is the horse can choose. I would not restrain Quincy or prevent him from moving. I believe that desensitizing a hose is about giving him enough time to understand that there is nothing to fear. The horse needs to decide that for himself. I don't use the old methods like tying the horse down and forcing him to accept the bag; that never works to gain a horse's trust. Quincy was so powerful and quick that if he was driven to the point of actual flight, he would do anything to get away—even if that meant harming the trainer or himself in the process.

When I brought out the plastic bag, I quickly realized that I would need more length than the twelve-foot lead rope I was using. I switched to a twenty-two-foot rope to allow Quincy the room to move away to where he felt safe. I would then begin the approach and retreat method.

I introduced the bag on the stick, and Quincy tried every trick he knew, including rearing, striking and bolting to avoid even being near the plastic bag. The session went on for two hours of agony, and at the end, he was no closer to acceptance than when we had started.

For the next two days, I played with Quincy; he continued to be a mental challenge and a puzzle to me. After hours of sweat and resistance, resulting in exhaustion for both of us, there was still no progress. I couldn't believe how strong-willed that horse was. He would stand, appearing to be okay, then suddenly his eyes would become wide with fear, nostrils flared, and he would rear and bolt. After I resisted all his tricks and finally got him to stand still, there still remained a look in his eye that seemed to say, "Do you want to do it again, cowboy? Because I'm game." His endurance and determination were like nothing I had ever experienced in a horse.

Quincy's future looked more and more desolate as the hours crawled by. Karen had watched all the sessions, and it became evident that he would never be the reliable trail horse she was hoping for. On that third and final day, I could see the disappointment on her face that mirrored how I was feeling too. Neither of us wanted to talk about what would become of Quincy. She left him there to return in the morning with her trailer.

I couldn't sleep that night. All I could do was lie awake thinking about that grey horse. What was to become of Quincy? How could I help him? What more could I do?

It kept pressing on my mind how fast he could react. Quincy could instantly perceive everything, even things I was completely unaware of. A measly rock on the ground would send this horse into a complete frenzy. As he bolted from the rock, a rope hanging off the fence would suddenly grab his attention and become a cougar waiting to pounce. He would go from object to object in the chaotic flight mode with never-ending stamina.

I thought to myself, *What if I can find a way to direct that energy and impulsion? What if I can get Quincy to watch me as closely as he watches everything else? Imagine what we could do! Could he be the ultimate performance horse?*

I thought, *If I can have success with this horse, and get him to the point where he is no longer dangerous, imagine what I will have learned in the process.* All of the great horsemen I admired had that one special horse they took the time to really connect with. Maybe Quincy was meant to be that horse for me. Maybe Quincy was my ultimate teacher.

Then I thought of Karen. I really wanted her to have a horse that was right for her. I had this one gelding, Chester. He was a big level-headed chestnut that I could do anything with. I COULD ALWAYS RELY ON CHESTER, whether I was starting out on the trail, cantering circles in the arena or packing around little kids for a pony ride. What if Karen could have success with him? Excited about the possibilities, I talked about an idea with my wife, Angie. The next day Karen and I made a deal.

I wanted a fresh start with Quincy. I tried to put a whole new foundation on him and create a partnership.

During the next few years, my sessions with Quincy continued to be a roller coaster. In the beginning. I could only ride him bareback. He reared with predictable regularity in such an extreme manner that when he reared, I would slide off, work out the issue on the ground, then jump back on. This was the only way to handle him. Our sessions almost always ended with both of us exhausted and in a sweat.

Quincy taught me the importance of a warm-up session. If he had more than a week off, I needed to be prepared to give him at least the first three days to get back into the groove. On the first day, I would offer no opinion about his reactions. I had to let him sort himself out. The second day would be similar, but with a little less response and a bit more control. By the third day, we had moments of connection, and by day four, we were ready to actually think about progressing in our training. It was a huge lesson learned about the timing of when you can ask more of a horse.

Twenty minutes of warm-up were still necessary at the beginning of the session, but I had the most fantastic connection with him, and he was open and ready to learn. There would still be the odd spook and reaction, a thought of a rear, but I could ask him to carry on, and he would. These were the moments that gave me hope. He was starting to let go of the fights of his past.

We were building a genuine partnership. I began to ask a little more of Quincy, but immediately I could feel some of the old resentment start to come back. He began to fight new exercises and would resort to his old tricks. It was really telling when I would go to his pasture to catch him, and he would walk the other way. It was at that point I decided not to push him.

It was enough for Quincy to just get back to zero. When I acquired him, he was so far in the negative that now it was satisfying enough to have him be a reasonably normal horse. He had overcome so much—his rearing was rare, and he could even accept a plastic bag anywhere on or around him.

It was at this point I decided to leave it at that. Regrettably, I realized I would have to let go of my dreams of Quincy becoming a performance horse. To bring him to that level of training was not in his best interest.

The story could have easily ended here, and I would have been proud of our accomplishments.

A few months later, however, I was on my way back from a client and stopped at the Quilchena Ranch in Merritt, BC. Cattle needed to be moved the following morning, and I was asked to help. I knew it would be a long day, and all of my other horses would not have the stamina. I looked at Quincy and thought, *Stamina? That's his middle name!* As I lay in bed that night, I thought about all the struggles we had been through and questioned whether he was ready for this.

By morning I was sure I needed to try. I wanted to give him that chance. As we headed down the trail, I could sense Quincy was very aware of everything around us. I was equally aware of what he could do, so I trod very lightly for the first few miles.

There was so much action with the cattle, dogs and cowboys; it was a lot to take in. The cow boss was aware of the challenges Quincy and I had faced in the past, and he didn't want me to get hurt if we were put in a tight situation. He gave me the longest possible circle to keep Quincy from the pressure situations close to the herd.

As the day wore on, Quincy became more and more comfortable and even seemed to be enjoying himself. When a calf broke loose from the herd, Quincy chased after it with so much intensity and turned so fast that he even surprised me. I felt a moment of absolute unity with him—for the first time ever!

Quincy came through for me that day. It became clear that he thrived when he had a purpose. Out on the ranch, we had a job to do; I relied on him, and he knew it. For the first time ever, Quincy wasn't saying, "Why me?" Instead, he was saying, "What's next?" It was an unbelievable feeling.

From that day forward, I made a deal with Quincy— that I would only ride him when I had a real purpose in mind. Unfortunately, the times became far and few between when I actually had a chance to take Quincy to a ranch or somewhere similar. I figured that if I was going to ride this horse again, I would need to create a little purpose—a series of exercises to give him that "reason why" within the arena.

My role as a teacher and trainer is to recognize the horse is an individual. You have to adapt to every situation. There was no horse finer than Quincy to bring that lesson home.

I had seen a Spanish rider on YouTube performing a fascinating bullfighting training exercise with a long pole as fate would have it. As he rode at a beautifully collected, slow canter, he held on to the end of the pole while the other end pivoted on the ground. This elegantly executed demonstration looked extremely difficult and complex, which enticed me even more to give it a try. I also thought this would be perfect for Quincy.

The next day I went to the local lumberyard and bought a twelve-foot coat rail.

That afternoon I saddled Quincy, mounted up and grabbed the pole. I dropped the end of the pole on the ground and asked Quincy to circle around it as I rested the other end in my hand. Quincy got it. He arched his neck and moved around and under the pole. At that very moment, Quincy and I became one. This collected, purpose-driven exercise caused Quincy to once again find motivation. He loved the pole even more than the cows, and I had a renewed feeling that this horse and I could really do something together.

It was a complete fluke that we had found Quincy's true calling. He even started meeting me at the gate again. Not only did this purpose-driven program completely change my partnership with Quincy, but it also improved my relationships with all my other horses. I developed an entire training program around the idea of purpose and giving a horse that powerful reason why.

A few months later, during a seminar at the Mane Event Expo, I explained to the audience how finding that purpose can provide a horse with so much motivation. I rode Quincy for an hour to demonstrate the impact that purpose can have on a horse. I even showed a few manoeuvres with the pole, and the audience loved it.

Susanna introduced herself after the demonstration and explained that she raised bullfighting horses in Spain. She was so blown away by Quincy's story and our demonstration that she offered to teach me more manoeuvres with the pole. With her help, I learned how to properly hold the pole and teach Quincy to spin underneath it. As a gift, Susanna also gave me a *forcado*, a proper bullfighting pole that she brought from Spain. My demonstration was so well received that I was asked by the Mane Event coordinators to make this "Spanish Dance" into a performance. They wanted Quincy to become part of the Saturday night "Equine Experience." I was thrilled.

I immediately said yes (of course); about five minutes later, I was wondering what I had just gotten myself into. It was one thing to have Quincy in a clinic situation but performing a five-minute routine in front of 3,000 plus people was another story.

Quincy and I practiced our routine with an elevated level of focus, and finally, the evening arrived. As I stood with Quincy just outside the gate, I could hear the cheering crowd. As the announcer introduced us, I could feel an anxious Quincy balling up underneath me. *Oh no,* I thought, *this is not a good time to rear.* I had the pole in my hand; people were swirling all around us behind the gate; we were just about to perform in front of thousands of people full of expectation. I reached down, gave Quincy a rub and said, "It's okay, bud." With one squeeze, he stepped right out there. He trusted me.

In the beginning, we started out slow and intentional, maybe even a bit jittery. As the intensity of the show grew. I was only aware of my horse underneath me. Quincy and I were so connected at that moment that I could not tell where he stopped and I began. I had never asked so much of a horse and gotten so much in return. That show and the feelings I had will stick with me forever. He and I walked out of the arena to a standing ovation. I could not have been prouder of him.

A few days later, I drove to our newly purchased ranch, nestled in the beautiful Nicola Valley just west of Merritt, BC. After a trip into town, I made it home just as the sun descended over the mountains behind the ranch. I had a spontaneous desire to see the full majesty of the sunset. I parked my truck, looked over to the corral, and there was that grey horse. I knew that if I was going to see the sun go down, he was the horse to take.

We left the yard at an eye-watering gallop. I knew if we went the right way, we could get to the top of the mountain quickly enough to catch the last glimpse of the sun. A couple of miles away from the ranch, I slowed Quincy to an extended trot. He was still ready and willing to gallop, but I thought we should take it easy. We went down the logging road, snaking along a small trail and charged up another logging road.

I noticed a small saddle between two mountains where it would be our only chance to drink in the sunset before the sun totally sank on the horizon. We went for it. The path dwindled away to nothing but solid brush. The forest was so dense and steep that I jumped off, and side by side, Quincy and I climbed and crashed through the thicket. We scrambled up the last hundred yards to the clearing.

Finally, we reached the top; the sun was still entirely in view. Both of us drenched in sweat, Quincy and I watched the sun disappear below the blue cast of the mountain ridge. I knew right then that I had achieved everything I had ever wanted to with Quincy.

I will never forget that moment for the rest of my life. Quincy had become more than I could ever have hoped. Quincy had become a true partner.

Jonathan Field's Accomplishments

- Contributing writer to nine different equestrian magazines

- Author of *The Art of Liberty Training for Horses*

- Producer of five horse training videos

- Recipient of many awards, including the 2010 Reader's Choice Award from *Equine Consumers' Guide*

Jonathan continues to offer clinics along with making film, television and radio appearances.

The Horse Who Found Me

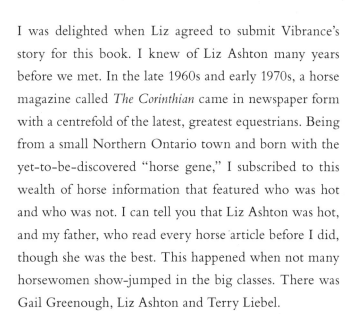

Dr. Liz Ashton and Vibrance

I was delighted when Liz agreed to submit Vibrance's story for this book. I knew of Liz Ashton many years before we met. In the late 1960s and early 1970s, a horse magazine called *The Corinthian* came in newspaper form with a centrefold of the latest, greatest equestrians. Being from a small Northern Ontario town and born with the yet-to-be-discovered "horse gene," I subscribed to this wealth of horse information that featured who was hot and who was not. I can tell you that Liz Ashton was hot, and my father, who read every horse article before I did, though she was the best. This happened when not many horsewomen show-jumped in the big classes. There was Gail Greenough, Liz Ashton and Terry Liebel.

After graduating from Grade 12, I needed to escape from New Liskeard, Ontario. I had applied to a few colleges with the idea that I would go wherever I was accepted. I attended the two-year horsemanship program at Humber College in Rexdale. I was thrilled to discover that Liz Ashton was involved with the course. She was short in stature, but appeared to be at least five foot ten in my eyes. I came from a small town and her presence filled my expectations. She was hired as an associate dean with a thirst for horse facts. I noticed she attended most of my classes, taking notes and learning as much as she could about the subjects taught. Not only was she brilliant, but she also had brawn with her muscular, athletic stature. During the summer between my two years at Humber, I worked for Jim Day (Olympian in Mexico 1968 Olympics, Show Jumping) at Sam-Son Farm, where Liz showed up again. There was a connection between her and this horse farm. During my research for this book, I learned that Ernie Samuels, who owned Sam-Son Farm, was helping Liz out with mounts for competition. Jim Day had been a friend of Liz's during their years in Pony Club and after. I remember her running to keep fit and her intellectual conversations with Jim Day, whom I considered a God. Many years after Humber, I ran into her again, briefly, at Nick Holmes-Smith's eventing site. I competed in my first Federation Equestrian International Competition in the Preliminary One Star Division. I was surprised that she remembered me, but do you expect anything else from someone like Dr. Liz Ashton?

Liz's sensitivity toward this horse touched me the most about this story. No matter how highly regarded Liz is, or what her education and experiences are, what lies underneath it all is a passion and talent for horses. As

Vibrance tells you *his* story, you can see him grow up before your eyes. He shows you what it is like to view the world with the wonderment of a young, inexperienced horse who turns into a showjumper.

How it all began!

Liz Ashton:

Everyone needs to unwind from daily life, and the best way I like to do that is by surfing the "horses for sale" website on my computer. My life's work and opportunities have changed, but my passion for horses and the sport of show jumping stays consistent. I certainly didn't need another horse, as I had two lovely jumpers living in the bottom of my house. The term "strange bedfellows" is no more accurate than when you have your stable directly below your bedroom.

I've always had that deep desire to find that special equine I would connect with: that single horse who would stand out and perform like no other. This thought leads me to continue browsing the myriad of horses listed on the web. At any moment, there are 3000 horses on the sites I peruse. Searching for horses is one of my favourite mind games. I needed to narrow my search requirements, and since my interest is in jumpers and Dutch Warmbloods, I concentrated on that criterion. I have knowledge of Dutch Warmbloods and their bloodlines; I felt confident in my ability to decide which individuals were promising and which ones were not worth a second look. To further narrow my field, I also wanted a horse who was young enough to train, so I inputted one of my search options as, "under five years old," with a price range of under $15,000.00. I am slightly under the average for height at five-two, so I didn't want a large horse. I further narrowed down my search to horses around sixteen hands high. Thankfully, that brought up twenty-five horses, which was a nice number for a short mental diversion. As I clicked on their pictures, I daydreamed about what each horse would be like. My learned eye critiqued their conformation and features, concluding whether each specimen had any talent and guessing at what their mind would be like. A talented horse with a crazy mind is not worth your time. The mentality of a horse is almost impossible to judge by looking at a picture or video on the computer.

Over the next few evenings, I was drawn to the "Warmbloods for Sale" website, and each time the same horse would capture my attention. This horse was a four-year-old Dutch Warmblood chestnut gelding by the stallion Burggraaf out of a Calvados mare. The colt's name was Vibrance. I kept going back to the short video of the youngster free jumping over a pair of barrels and a pole. His ears were pricked and focused on the obstacle before him. He seemed to be playing back and forth with this task that must have seemed strange to him. When I looked at his face and saw the expression in his eyes, I thought the name Vibrance was well suited. I was drawn to him and could see myself working with this enthusiastic youngster. My growing excitement enticed me to call my husband into the room to see the video, as I valued his approval of my find. Much to my surprise, he also liked what he saw. Within an instant, the phone was in my hand, and I was dialing the number listed on the website. My head was full of questions about this horse—first, was he still for sale. I found out that the colt was not yet under saddle. The owner was trying to decide whether to sell the horse at a lower cost or hire a professional trainer to start him under saddle. Before I knew it, I had made a deal, and this vibrant young horse was about to have a new home.

It was late July, and I needed to make arrangements to have him shipped from his home in Maryland, Virginia, to Victoria, British Columbia. Vibrance first arrived in Toronto and he was then driven across Canada. It was a long trip for Vibrance and a challenging time for me as I waited to get the first glimpse of my new show jumping partner. The days and hours dragged by, as I waited for my horse to arrive.

Buying a horse is always a gamble. Sometimes you win, but sometimes you lose and the horse you chose is not at all what you think they are going to be. I was worried, hoping that no harm would come to him and that he would travel well. So much to consider and obsess about. I just wanted him here and safe.

Vibrance's Letter to Home:

Hi Mom,

I was put in the trailer this morning to travel a long distance away from home. There were other non-familiar horses in the trailer with me. I miss the comfort and warmth of my stall. After seemingly endless hours, I was unloaded in Western Canada. My legs were tired from adjusting to the rock, stop and go of the horse van. I was curious about this new place, but my senses told me that I would not be here for long. I didn't recognize any humans busying themselves to get us food and water.

I looked down the alleyway of the barn and saw a lady and a gentleman coming up to the opening in my stall door. The lady was very excited while she looked me over. I had a sense that she knew me by the tone of her voice. This was all a mystery to me, as I knew that I had not met her before. As the two of them patted me, I felt that I would not be returning to you, and this new lady would be taking over my care.

The next day, I was loaded onto my new owner's horse van, beside her horse, Lieber. She had brought this horse to keep me company on the trip. Lieber told me all about my new home and explained that we would become stablemates. My new owner, as you probably know, is Liz Ashton. Lieber spoke highly of Liz and told me she was an accomplished horsewoman. He said that she was kind and fair. She would teach me many new things that would challenge my mind and body. I had an adventure ahead of me.

The truck and trailer were driven onto a ferry. We were packed on all sides with vehicles. Then there was the most exciting sensation. The horse track was not moving, but I could feel a roll and pitch through my hooves. Lieber told me that he had been on the ferry before, and it would not be long before we would drive off and travel to my new home. He said I would live on an island that is beautiful and lush with vegetation. Most important, there would be much succulent grass.

Once we were off the ferry, it was a comfortable drive to the farm. I backed off the trailer and looked around. My new home is lovely, and there are other horses to get to know besides Lieber. The whole place was designed with horses in mind. Even the house my people live in was built over the stable. Amazing!

The following day, I was led to my own turn-out paddock. Everything was so different; I just wanted to drink it all in. I was scared, anxious and curious, all wrapped up in one. Lieber, and the other horse, Tore, were in a paddock together, but too far away for me to rub noses and talk to them. I had a good look at my paddock's fence. It wasn't that high, maybe coming up to the base of my neck. I thought that if I could get a little run at it, I could probably clear it. As it turns out, there was just enough room for me to trot and jump over the rails. Liz, who must have been watching from the house, came running out with a carrot to fetch me. She tried to be angry, but I could see a glint in her eye and knew she was pretty proud of my enthusiasm. She put me in Tore's adjoining paddock to have company. We visited over the fence, rubbed each other's withers with our noses, and got to know each other.

My next adventure was to have a bath. Why is it that humans think that we should be clean? The water was warm, and before I knew it, I was rinsed and a polar fleece blanket was placed over my back. As Liz fussed and worked, she said things like I would become a show horse. She planned to put my jumping skills to good use when we travel to competitions. I was caught up in her words when I felt an uncomfortable sensation at the top of my mane. Liz was pulling my hair out to make my mane shorter and more even. I want to impress my new friends, but these braids were put in my hair, making me feel like a sissy. She explained that all this primping up was part of becoming a show horse.

All in all, I really like it here. There is good quality hay and oats to eat. The carrots that I love so much are given out regularly. I am going to miss you back in the United States. Thanks for giving me a good start in life and finding such a good owner.

Love,

Vibrance

P.S. Give my old friends a pat on the neck and say goodbye for me.

Vibrance's Diary

August 07, 2006

I slept well last night. When I glanced up, I saw Lieber standing in his stall, looking over me. I remembered when I was a young colt, my mother used to stand over me, and I could feel the hot breath from her nostrils bathing me. Lieber was protecting me like my mother used to. Knowing that I am not alone and have close friends is comforting.

There was no chance of my life becoming routine, as the very next day, I was loaded onto the trailer and taken over to the neighbours. Liz, Tore and Lieber were going away to a ten-day horse show, and Liz didn't want me to be left alone. *What the heck?* I had just gotten used to my new home, and now I've been sent to another location; my new friends have left, and I have to get used to four more horses. At first, I really wanted to jump this fence and go home!

On the other hand, I now face fifteen acres of horse-friendly pasture. This farm is called "Hunt Valley," although I don't see any foxes. That is what horses and hounds hunt, right?

September 2006

Every day brings new changes. Liz bought me my own saddle and bridle. She is very good at knowing how to get me used to the latest equipment. There are many straps and buckles, but nothing hurts me or flaps in my face, so I wasn't afraid.

The saddle felt comfortable, along with the piece of leather around my belly called a girth. Liz put her foot in the stirrup, climbing up on my back. Wow, that was different. I am glad she is not very big. She shuffled her weight from side to side, and I felt unstable, like a young colt who was standing up for the first time. Not only does her weight put me out of balance, but it is also a strange feeling having her head above mine. I have watched her ride the other horses and felt jealous that I was omitted. This is my big debut, and I am pleased to be part of the big boys' club.

My schooling days start with Liz putting me on a nylon strip called a lunge line. I have to run around in a circle with Liz in the middle. She calls out words to me. I am not sure what they mean, but I will get the hang of it with patience and time. After twenty minutes, Liz climbs on and steers me around the ring. I can feel her hands on the ends of the reins, gently turning the bit in my mouth. Her legs caress my sides. Walking is easy but trotting while balancing her weight is more complicated. I want to just let loose and run, but Liz gently pulls on the reins and tells me that I can't go any faster when I get excited.

After my outing each day, I get groomed while being cross-tied in the alley of the barn. Tore is a real character. Today, Liz was grooming one side, and I felt a strange sensation on the other side. It felt like I was being stroked with a sponge, but instead, it was Tore licking my side. He must have liked the salt in my coat.

At the end of the day, we get tucked in our stalls, with good food, fresh carrots and a clean bed of shavings. Life is good.

October 2006

As Liz calls it, my "schooling" sessions are getting longer, and I get to run or canter. Each day she asks new things from me, and I am starting to learn what it means when she uses her legs, hands and body weight. I can't help but see a difference in my body. Plentiful food has put some healthy weight on my bones. My coat is shiny, and the work has started to build muscle on my neck, back and haunches. I am proud of my new look, and I can see a sense of pride in Liz when she looks at me. She spends more time with my care and tells me that I am special. Look out, Tore and Lieber, because I am on my way.

My name has got to be a topic of discussion around the farm. Liz started out calling me Vibee, for short, but Liz's friends call her Libby. I guess the names sounded too similar, so my stable name has been changed to Pewee. Why don't they just call me Vibrance? I guess that name will be reserved for when I go to the shows.

One day, a large trailer drove into the yard, and a beautiful mare unloaded, strutting her stuff in front of us. Her name was Marlo, and she belonged to the Island's jumping legend, Eddie Macken. I tried to get to know her, but she was a snob. She was proud of what her owner had accomplished in his riding career. Well, I'd never heard of Eddie, but my owner Liz has been on the Canadian Olympic Team, and I am definitely proud of her. Now that we both had things to brag about, I hope that we could put our differences aside and be friends. As it turns out, we were paddock mates at Hunt Valley, while Liz was away with Lieber and Tore.

Marlo shared her experiences in the show ring. There is so much I will have to get used to. She talked about the crowds and the noise. Every time I go into the show ring, there will be jumps that I will not be familiar with, and I'll have to go into the ring alone; there won't be another horse there to keep me supported. Thank goodness I have Liz to guide me through the maze of jumps. Marlo taught me a lot, and in the end, I was sorry to see her go.

Once I returned home, it was back to daily training. I can't understand why I am not jumping yet. Liz keeps telling me that I have to wait until my body catches up with my mind. I have already shown her that I can jump fences without her, so why can't I jump in the practice arena with her? I just know that this is something that I will be good at. It looks like so much fun.

The weather has started to get cooler. I am very impressed with my growing wardrobe. Every time the temperature outside changes, I get a new blanket. Scuttlebutt has it that there is a blanket for every season and even a rain sheet to keep me dry. I wonder if Liz's wardrobe is as colour-coordinated as mine? It is a lot of work for the grooms to put my outerwear on and off when I have a fur coat of my own, but in saying that, I am thankful to be warm and dry.

I don't feel like an outsider anymore. This is my home, and I feel like one of the boys.

November 2006

I can't tell you how beautiful it is here. Beside our practice ring is a small pond teeming with wildlife. I have become familiar with a rather large bird with long skinny legs. This blue heron thinks that the pond has been stocked primarily for him. The poor little goldfish don't stand a chance when he stabs the water with his long pointy beak.

The blue heron likes to fly off his rock when one of us comes into the ring to school. Tore and Lieber really dislike this stately creature and make a big deal of him. They like to cry foul and whirl at the sight of him. I just don't see what the big deal is. As a matter of fact, I find this magnificent creature rather interesting.

Training is moving along well, and I have learned to organize my four legs over poles on the ground. The poles are spaced evenly, so it doesn't take me long to figure it out. Liz gives me time to look at the new task; she walks me through it and eventually asks me to trot. Before long, I have my self-assurance and am forging ahead with long, fluid movements. I have confidence in my rider, and we continuously learn about each other every day.

The weather is changing again, and I'd noticed that my coat had become thick and woolly. With the exertion of training, my hair gets wet with sweat, and it takes a long time to dry. Liz decided that my long, warm coat was coming off. Humans have a strange desire to change what is natural. Tore told me that the clippers were large, ticklish, noisy, and they would become hot as time went on. Each blade swipe removed a path of hair, exposing my cool skin. I wished I could say, "Hurry up and finish so I can get my blanket on!"

I get a few days off as Liz travels to Toronto. She returns and then travels up the Island for a few days. My training has been intense, and with this break, Liz says it is time for me to "as-si-mi-late" what I have learned, whatever that means.

Andrea, my groom, has come to take care of us. She is always accompanied by her two large dogs. However, our dog Laurel is not amused with these new visitors that have come to share his property. It won't be long before Liz returns and things return to normal.

December 2006

I am getting bolder; I am bigger by one inch and stronger. My newly shaved coat shines with brilliance. I don't see why I have to follow so many rules. This stable has too many stipulations on what a horse can or cannot do. I love feeding time, but Tore, who lives on the other side of the wall, sticks his nose over the partition. There is no way that he is going to get my food. I don't want him to climb over and get my hay with the way he can jump. I need to let him know that I am no pushover, so I retaliate by slamming my body into the wall, and in doing so, I make lots of noise. It works. I feel a strong desire to protect my food at every feeding, so I keep practicing my body slam. Liz gets mad at me and tells me how foolish I am. Maybe if she loved her food like I love mine, she would understand.

On a happy note, my training has taken a giant leap forward! It all came about when Liz was riding me while Andrea rode Tore. We did the mandatory trotting poles, but then the poles were put up in the form of an" X." I could no longer just trot; I had to somehow get over the raised poles. Tore led the way, and I could see him make a leap. Before I knew it, I was faced with the same obstacle and had to do something, so I leaped over it as well. Liz was very excited and made a fuss over me. This was it. This was the moment I had been waiting for. I was jumping. We went over the raised poles many times, and by the end of that day, I had reason to be very proud of myself. This was fun and easy.

As the next few days progressed, the "X" was made into a vertical pole, which required that I make more of an effort. Liz praised me with each new skill and changed up the difficulty. Finally, I was allowed to canter a small course of jumps. I was thrilled with myself and wanted to show Liz how happy I was by adding a few bucks and twirls, but she would not let me get carried away. I know that Liz has lots of experience, but I can make this training much more fun for both of us with my new knowledge. She should let me do as I please and not have so much control.

It is Christmastime, and I feel like I have been here all of my life. My stall has been fancied up with tinsel, and I have my very own stocking hung by my stall door, albeit, just out of reach. I have been told that if I am nice and not naughty, there will be carrots and apples on Christmas Day from Santa Claus. Reindeer are just horses with antlers, right? I bet that I could pull the sleigh if asked to, especially if Liz was there to direct me!

The change of season brought a new mare into our little herd with the name "Plus Que Parfait." I learned that she came from Ottawa, Ontario, in the same van I came on five months ago. She's a lovely bay mare, nine years old with big brown eyes and is Dutch bred, like me. I really would like to get close to her, but Tore has let me know that all the girls in the barn belong to him. He is older, wiser, and thinks I am too young to have a girlfriend. Too young! I will be five in just over a week. I hope they have ordered a carrot cake for my birthday.

January 2007

This was the day and month my life changed. I was watching Liz as she busied herself packing the trailer. Initially, I thought she was taking Parfait and Lieber to a show, and I would be left at home again. But what was that she was carrying? It was my saddle and bridle. She gave me a glance as she walked by, and I could swear that she winked at me. I couldn't believe it! I was heading out with my stablemates to my first show. My ears were forward, and I followed Liz's every move expectantly as she went back and forth carrying supplies to the truck. I could hardly contain my excitement.

We were off to the HITS (Horse Shows in the Sun) at Thermal, California, for three weeks. It was a long ride, so I was glad that my two stablemates were there to keep me company. We stopped twice on the way. Once in Oregon and once in Northern California. California was hot and sunny. The nights were cold, but Liz had packed our warm blankets.

As the horse trailer drove into the competition grounds, I could see many more horses. There were people everywhere. Looking out the tiny window of my trailer stall, I could see flags and piles of jumps in the outdoor arenas. "Let me out of here so I can explore all the sights and sounds!" Lieber and Parfait were much calmer than I, but then they had done this before.

I was backed out of the trailer, and Liz let me look around a little bit, but then I was led into a barn with endless stalls in it. A horse could never get bored here. There were busy humans around unloading their horse gear, setting up stalls for tack rooms, tacking up their horses to go out for a schooling session.

Liz explained to me that I was just here for the experience. I wasn't going to actually compete. I would get to go into the warm-up ring and practice what I had learned at home. After Lieber and Parfait went out to exercise, it was my turn. We entered a ring with many horses going around in circles. I saw jumps set up in the middle, so I had to be careful; it felt like organized confusion. I was nervous, but Liz had things well in hand. Although my surroundings were new, Liz gave me the same commands as she did at home. I felt confident in her guidance and realized that the work was the same. She pointed me at the jumps in the middle of the ring, and I knew what to do. After a few days of practicing in the ring, Liz took me into the main arena for some complete jump courses, but there was no pomp and circumstance. These were called practice rounds. I felt much more at ease. So, this is what it is like to be at a show!

It was the second week at Thermal, and Liz was spending more time grooming me. She left and came back with my saddle, but she was all dressed in her show clothes. I couldn't believe it. Was I actually going to be going into the show ring? I had seen it at a distance. The warm-up ring was familiar to me, and I limbered up well. A man called a number, and sure enough, Liz headed over to the entrance gate of the show ring. The whole time I was thinking, *Lieber, where are you? I could really use your company right now!*

I trotted into the ring all by myself and halted, facing a man sitting on an elevated platform. I am not sure if Liz knew him, but they nodded to each other. A buzzer went, and we started to circle to the first obstacle. The jumps were brightly coloured and fancied up with flowers and trees. I was a little unsure, but Liz gave me clear aids with her legs to encourage me. I had negotiated so many jumps at home that I knew what was expected of me. Before I knew it, we had sailed over twelve jumps, and Liz guided me out of the ring. The crowd clapped, and I felt proud of my accomplishment. Liz patted my neck, and I knew that she was pleased with me. What a day.

We went into the show ring several times to compete at the Level One, Three-Foot-High Division. I cantered the individual jumps competently for an inexperienced, green horse. I found it easy, and Mum couldn't believe how smoothly I manoeuvred the courses. I want to come back next year.

March 2007

We left Thermal, California, behind and returned to Victoria. During the long trip home, my head was swirling with all the new experiences. I have to admit that I am tired. My body and legs are weary, and my brain has taken in more information than riding students at a clinic. The next time we go to a show, I will not feel intimidated.

It was good to be home and have some time off. I can't help wondering when our next adventure will come. It is good to know that I won't be left home anymore. I have graduated and am now a "showjumper."

May 2007

My stablemates seem to change regularly. I was saddened to find out that I was going to lose Lieber. We travelled to Washington for a show, and Lieber was dropped off in Vancouver. He was going to his new Toronto home. Lieber got off the van. I called him and he called back, but I knew that we would not see each other again. He was the first horse I met when I came here, and we had a good time playing together, so I will miss him. I hope that I will not be shipped off and not see Liz or my friends again.

The show in Washington was a huge event, and it was the first time that I competed internationally. There were horses there from all over North America. As I looked around, I concluded that I was one of the youngest. Liz got sick the first night that we arrived. Dad said that she had food poisoning, and it would take a day or two before she could train us. He took us for walks to get us familiar with the competition site. The trainer across the hallway in the barn thought Dad was pretty special and said he should get the "husband of the year award" for being so attentive.

Liz returned to health and gave me my first taste of international competition. The jumps were well placed, and I jumped my heart out. There was so much to look at, sometimes it was hard to hold my focus. I have learned that if you don't knock down any poles on the first round, all the horses that went clear qualify to perform in the jump-off. Liz let me go a little faster the second time around, but my natural talent is how quickly I can turn.

Once we returned from Washington, we were off to a competition close to home. The man who designed the jump course was an international course designer, so he presented each horse and rider with unique challenges. It was the first time that I jumped on the grass. With each push off the ground, it felt like the sod slipped away under my hooves. It was time for me to get some special shoes.

We were only home one day when the blacksmith drove up in his truck with a box that made a fire on the back end of it. I was used to the farrier, but his banging on metal was unnerving. He picked up my foot and placed the hot metal shoe on it. A cloud of smoke swirled around my head. What a stink! After he cooled the shoe, he proceeded to bang my foot and attach the shoe with nails. Are you kidding me? The procedure was strange, but it didn't hurt, so I allowed him to finish the job. Apparently, Liz can screw metal studs in the bottom of the shoe to have better traction on grass. Okay, I can live with that.

The news around the barn was that we were going to Spruce Meadows in Calgary, Alberta, and I would have to jump on grass again. Spruce Meadows sounded impressive, high-class. This would not be Tore's or Parfait's first trip to this prestigious event. They told me that it was stressful, but I was not afraid to be truthful. Stress does not affect me.

Spruce Meadows was exciting. It was just as Marlo had described to me when we were together. There were crowds of people everywhere. The jumps were inviting and colourful. No matter where we went, there was one constant in my life, and that was Liz. She guided me around the courses, and every time we went into the ring, I was getting better. Jumping has to do a lot with timing and getting to that sweet spot to jump from. If I missed that spot, I would have to jump long, or I would have to make a shuffle step to get over the obstacle. Liz has a great eye, and she tries to help me, but sometimes there is so much going on I just don't hear her. We did well in Spruce Meadows, and I earned some ribbons and money for my effort. When the ribbon was presented to me, I could feel the pride in Liz. I so much want to please her. She says that I have all kinds of raw talent, but I need to get it more under control.

I train, travel and play with my friends, so my life is complete. I tend to spend too much emotional and physical energy on my schooling exercises, so I am exhausted by the end of the day. There is nothing to fear here, so I feel comfortable enough to lie flat with my legs stretched as far as they will go. I can rest this way for hours. I hear that we are off on another road trip tomorrow, so I had better be ready.

January 2008

This is the start of a new year, and I need to make some New Year's resolutions. Now that I am a year older, my owner and groom would like me to be a better-behaved boy. I find grooming so dull. There has to be a way to make it more interesting. Have you ever noticed what a horse can do with his lips? My upper lip acts like a short trunk, capable of wiggling and contorting into various shapes. I have been practicing the art of sucking articles into my mouth. The lead shank is handy, and if you play with it long enough, it usually becomes undone. If a horse is lucky, no one will notice, and you can sneak down the hall and grab a mouthful of hay. My groom comes with an assortment of things to play with. There are her arms, fingers and pieces of clothing that can be tugged and pulled on. When I get told "No," which is an unacceptable answer to me, I dangle my tongue out the corner of my mouth. My people pretend to be disgusted with me, but I think they kind of enjoy my antics. That gets a smile every time. Sometimes they can't help themselves and pull on my tongue. When Lieber is around and we are turned out together, we accidently hurt each other's tongues, since there is nothing else to do but play.

One day there was a jar of cookies close to where I was being prettied up that had been given to us by my vet's daughter. I had watched several times as the lid of the jar was unscrewed, and I was given a treat. I only got one little morsel when there was so much in the container. I am a large horse, and I have a big appetite. I needed to bide my time until the right moment presented itself. My groom left me to get some fly spray from the tack room. This was my chance. I stretched my neck as far as my lead would allow and flicked the top of the container with my agile lips. One flick was followed by another. It was working, and I was getting closer to my prize. At that moment, my groom showed up and yelled my name. I made one last attempt, and the jar went crashing to the floor, spilling its precious contents. Liz was just walking into the barn and quickly retrieved the loot before I managed to obtain any of the cookies. I had been able to unscrew the lid, which impressed everyone.

My New Year's resolution to be better behaved will be a tough one. All I can say is that I will try.

April 2008

It has been wonderful to live in British Columbia. Let's see—I was conceived in Holland, born in America, and I am now living in the most beautiful place in Canada. I have competed in both North American countries and am looking forward to returning to California. I had so much fun last year. Some humans have not done what I have done. I am becoming quite the world traveller!

We are going to be away for three weeks. I am physically able to jump higher, and I am getting very clever in my approach to the jumps. My muscles are becoming more developed and my technique is improving. The noise and distractions take my attention less often. I can focus on the aids Liz is giving. We are becoming more of a team, but I still depend on her for direction and speed control.

Once I return from California, we are off to the Western Canadian Young Horse Championships at Thunderbird Show Park near Vancouver. I would like to go to the Canadian Championships in Toronto, but it is too far to travel for three classes. I know that I would do well if I could talk Liz into taking me. At least I get to jump at the Spruce Meadows Masters in Calgary, 1.2-Metre Division. Parfait will come with me to keep me company and compete. The hardest thing is the long miles in the horse trailer. It takes me one day to recover and get my bearings at the different venues.

Each competition gives me new jumps to negotiate, and the courses are becoming more complex. The footing changes from hard to soft, grassy to muddy, sandy to small pebbles. The constant change taxes my brain and tires out my legs. I wouldn't have it any other way when I think about it. I see horses that stand in their fields and never go anywhere. I feel sorry for them. They must be lonely and bored. Liz treats me like the athlete that I am. I get the best of personal care and feed. What more could you ask for?

October 2009

I enjoyed returning to Spruce Meadows. The stabling and grounds were familiar to me, and so was the pomp and circumstance surrounding such a big show. The competition was very tough! The other seventy entries were older than me. The course designers are known for making their courses corners tight. I rose to the challenge and did not have a single rail down. Liz thinks I am not experienced enough to add a lot of speed, so we received some time faults in two of my classes. She was pleased with me, and in turn, I was delighted with my performance.

Parfait and I went to the mainland for the BC Hunter Jumper Association Fall Finale when we got back home. These courses were a piece of cake after Spruce Meadows. I won all of my three 1.2-metre classes and was fifth in the 1.3-Metre Grand Prix. That was my first time jumping at that height. Parfait was also fantastic. She won all of her classes at 1.3 metres to become the champion of her division.

We are now at home with Tore for the fall and winter. It is fantastic that the grass is still green on the Island. After a tough show season, I can hardly wait to be out on the pasture. It is time to just be a horse and hang out with my buddies without expectations. We sometimes go out for a casual ride on the Lochside Trail. There is much to look at as the trail is used for many purposes. There are walkers, runners, cyclists, birdwatchers, and sometimes we have come across a horse-drawn carriage. Carriages make too much noise, and those horses can't jump anything with such bulk behind them.

January 2009

I didn't fill any of last year's resolutions regarding my behaviour, so I will not make any for this year. No matter how hard I try to be good, I find it entertaining to crowd my groom into the wall while getting my mouth on anything and everything, not to mention hanging my tongue out. My antics amuse those around me, which makes it all worthwhile. I work hard, and I play hard. There is nothing wrong with that.

I get antsy this time of year. There is a lot of rain, and sometimes there is snow. I miss the heron in the pond. I don't know where he goes for the winter, but sure enough, he will return in the spring. There is not much to do until I train for the next show season. The weather in Victoria will break soon, and Liz will get out to set up jump gymnastics in the outdoor arena. I bet she lies awake at night just thinking of combinations to make me better. For my part, I am practicing my turns, stops and sprinting while I am turned out in my paddock. Ho-hum. I could use a little excitement.

May 2009

It is good to get back into the swing of things. I have been training hard, and the show season is upon us. Parfait and I went back down to Thermal, California, to compete at the Horse Shows in the Sun. My bank account is growing. Jumping is one of the few horse sports that gives money for prizes. I was in the ribbons for most of my classes, and I placed second in the 1.3-Metre Classic. In all my classes combined, I earned $3,300.00.

When we got home, a new horse joined the barn. Liz takes on horses to train, and this new mare, Fancy Hill, will be going with us back to Spruce Meadows.

I didn't realize that Fancy was so good. She won the 1.4-Metre CN Cup. I couldn't be outdone by a mare, so I won the 1.3-Metre Ashcor Mini Grand Prix. It was no easy feat. There was a choice on the course, whether you went around a vertical jump to a very wide oxer or took the inside turn, which only gave a horse one stride to set up for the oxer. Liz knew that I could do it, and her confidence spurred me to give it all I had. A couple of other horses tried the inside turn and ended up crashing into the oxer. I was three seconds faster than the second-place horse, which is a lot. I earned $2,200.00 for that one class. At last, Liz is letting me use my speed.

I sometimes reflect on how far I have come since I have been with Liz. I started out not knowing where I was going or what my life would be like. Now I am a successful jumping horse. I could not do it if I didn't like to jump, but it tests me, and I like the challenge. The most important thing is my bond with Liz. I can't stress that enough. She is starting to trust me more and allow me to go faster. I am also paying closer attention to her guidance, which means I make fewer mistakes and use my turning talents.

I have heard that Liz is retiring at the end of June from her job as president of Camosun College. I am peaking in my performances, so this is a good time for Liz not to work. She will have more time for me, training and competing.

September 2009

This has been a fantastic year. I've learned so much about being a top competitor. I am much more focused, and I am growing up in my mental attitude. Jumping is still fun, but it is getting more demanding.

I jumped my first National Level Grand Prix in August at Calgary's Rocky Mountain Horse Show. I earned eighth place in the $50,000.00 Oil Patch Grand Prix. Although my first round was clear of faults, I had an unfortunate rail down on my second round. I was mad at myself for making that mistake. The season is coming to an end, and I am ready for the break.

My two travel mates have now left the barn. Parfait was sold in the summer and is living with a great family in Calgary. Fancy Hill has gone back to Ottawa. While in Calgary, Liz bought a young four-year-old gelding called Cando. I remember being that age and coming to this stable. I am now in the position of mentoring this new boy like I was mentored by Lieber and Tore, or I could teach him to be a brat. I will sleep on it and make a decision in the morning. I don't want to be the only bad boy in the barn.

Cando was not the only new horse that arrived. Aryanna, another Dutch Warmblood, came from Ottawa. Her sire is Voltair out of a Grannus mare. Tore reminded me that he was in charge of all mares, so I won't have much chance to befriend her. While Aryanna is learning to be ridden, Cando and I are great sparring partners over the fence. I have learned that pulling each other's tongues can be painful, so we have switched to pulling on each other's halters. This angers Liz because we have destroyed many headstalls, but I make my own money so she can pay for the new equipment out of my bank account. The game does keep us entertained.

December 2009

It is Christmas again, and I received the best present yet. Liz and Santa bought me a large orange buoy to play with. At first, I wasn't sure about this strange new toy.

It is a brightly coloured round ball with a handle on it, just the right size for my mouth. I snuck up on it, trying to see if it smelled like anything I knew. In doing so, I accidentally tapped it with my hoof, and it rolled away from me. The second time I went up to it, I hit it on purpose, so it moved even farther. What a great toy. Each day I get turned out, I search for my orange ball. Grabbing it by the handle with my mouth, I can rear up into the air and bounce it off the clouds. At least that is what it feels like. I can run with it, kick it, swing it around and not destroy it. Not only is it fun, but it is my exercise program. Liz says it is important to cross-train, and with my ball, this boy is going to be in great shape for the upcoming show season!

August 2010

Liz is now retired, so we could spend seven weeks down in California at the Horse Show in the Sun. By the time we returned home, we had missed all of the bad weather. I was now showing in the Division Four classes at the height of 1.4 metres. My skills were becoming perfected, but Liz's shoulder gave her trouble. She had injured her rotator cuff. The orthopedic surgeon said she tore the infraspinatus muscle totally and the supraspinatus muscle partially. Her shoulder cannot be repaired, and soft tissue takes a very long time to heal. Even though Liz has been going to physiotherapy, her strength and range of movement have been compromised. I feel a difference in my mouth as the symmetry between her two hands has changed. Liz has had severe back problems along with bad knees. I often hear her say that she is too old to jump and compete.

I sure hope we can continue competing together for a few more years. I love my job and my partnership with Liz. I have seen stablemates come and go, but I am sure that I am here to stay.

Liz Ashton (writing as Liz):

Pewee (Vibrance) and I have a great bond. It is time for him to take more responsibilities as he and I get older. I am fortunate that his training is such that we can still communicate and get the job done even with my weakened arm. Over the summer of 2011, we had our challenges. There were ups and downs. One of the ups was winning the Bow Valley Classic Open, Welcome Class, in May at Anderson Ranch in Calgary. We both seemed to get our act together, and it felt great. Later in the same year, on return to Anderson Ranch, Vibrance and I jumped the FEI (Federation Equestrian International) Division for the first time, and we were very competitive. The jumps were large, and Vibrance, at eight years old, was the youngest horse to compete in the International Division. To finish off a brilliant season, Vibrance won the Western Canadian Eight-Year-Old Young Horse Development Series and was once again Western Canadian Champion.

Horses are in my blood, and show jumping gives me a thrill that I cannot explain. Even as I age and my body is complaining, there is still the drive to continue. I am fortunate to have Vibrance in my life. The communication between us is so honed that sometimes I think he reads my mind. We will both carry on, and hopefully, we have a few more FEI classes in us.

Liz Ashton's Accomplishments

- 1969, 1970, 1972 Canadian Show Jumping Team on the Fall International Circuit

- 1975 Pan American Eventing Team, Mexico City

- 1976 Olympic Eventing Team, Montreal, Quebec

- 1978 World Championships Eventing Team, winning gold in Moscow, Russia

- 1980 Alternate Olympic Eventing Team, placing sixth individually

- 1984 Olympic Eventing Team, Los Angeles, California

During the years 1977–1992, Liz was a member of the National Coaching Committee; Level 3 Eventing Coach; member of the Athlete Advisory Council; Sports Weekend Colour Commentator for Show Jumping, *National Examiner for Pony Club,* Chairperson for the Canadian Equestrian Team—Eventing; High-Performance

Committee member; and on the Eventing Selection Committee.

- Inducted into the Pony Club Hall of Fame

- Director of Equine Studies at Humber College in Toronto

- Associate Dean of Applied and Creative Arts, Humber College

- Dean of Hospitality, Tourism and Leisure Management, Humber College

- VP Education, Sir Sandford Fleming College in Peterborough, Ontario

- President of Camosun College in Victoria, British Columbia

The First Few Hours

Joy Kimler

The light was starting to extend its fingers into the darkness. I could see my breath in the air from the warmth of my sleeping bag. It was time to get up; it was cross-country day. I had been checking my watch every ten minutes for what seemed like hours, as I went over the course, jump by jump, in my head. I was excited, not worried, except for that one jump at the back of the course. There was always one jump that commanded my attention.

I slipped down onto the camper benches, trying not to disturb the others. *Brrr,* it was cold. I need my heavy jacket and the mud-laden running shoes from yesterday. The door was noisy, so I did my best to open it quietly and then stepped out into the world.

There was little stirring as I turned around and drank in the ambiance of the competition site. The grounds were carefully manicured, much like a golf course but with cross-country jumps speckling the landscape. I felt a sense of peace in the air, which was in sharp contrast to what was inside of me. The trees stood majestic, with their leaves soft and manicured. The morning mist played hide and seek amongst the treetops and hills. I could not imagine being anywhere else at this moment, and I felt truly thankful for this experience. These few hours were the best part of the day, and the last time I would have any tranquility until after my ride.

I cuddled a few flakes of hay under my arm, heading toward the horses nestled in their small makeshift stalls. I could hear soft snorting and hooves rustling in the bedding. The familiar smell of all things horse was in the air. A few of them were calling to alert their riders that it was time to get going. Oh, yes, there were always a few that had escaped their pens no matter how craftily their gate was tied.

Most heads were down, but Donovan's black head was straight up, looking for me. He nickered quietly with his ears erect and his eyes wide open. He knew as well as I did what day this was. Donovan's expression is entirely different from yesterdays. He dislikes dressage, but he loves cross-country. Happy to receive the hay and fresh water, he plunged his muzzle into the flake, pulling out the best pieces. I had to walk my course one more time to collect my thoughts and secure my plan.

It was not until I retired from the sport that I realized how special the first few hours of competition day were. My heart was full of expectations both for my performance and for Donovan's. We were a team, and I had confidence in him.

At the end of my life, I will think of these first few hours on competition day. I will remember the quietness, beauty, expectation and the union I had with my horse. I will know in the depth of my soul that I was privileged.

Epilogue

When horse enthusiasts have not seen each other for a while, the first thing they ask is, "Are you still riding?" The answer is usually "Yes, of course."

As we mature in this sport, our focus can change. We become coaches, trail riders, breeders, or become involved in local equestrian groups. One does not cease to love horses, even when we are older and have broken bones or experienced other injuries. The thought of stopping is inconceivable, much to the disbelief and dismay of those who care about us.

There are times we have had to put a beloved horse down. We grieve for a while and then acquire a new exciting one, opening up a different chapter in our equine experience. Each horse brings its package of problems and talents, a puzzle that needs to be solved.

All of the contributors to *Heartfelt* have continued to ride and experience the wonder of this unique partnership. Most have gone on to teach others, as it would be a shame not to pass on the years of experience. I always say you cannot buy experience. We have spent a long time and plenty of patience to acquire this know-how.

Myself, I am entering my first working equitation show, as galloping over cross-country fences is not advised at my age. I am considering a follow-up to this book with more horse stories or possibly adventures from our canine population.

One thing is for sure, every story about the human-animal connection touches my heart and makes me yearn to hear and tell more.